the big **wheat &**
**gluten**
**free**
cookbook

# jody vassallo

baking recipes  dianne boyle

Grub Street • London

# contents

# introduction

There are a number of reasons why wheat and gluten products may be avoided in the diet. Most frequently it is people who suffer from coeliac (pronounced 'seeliac') disease who require a strict lifelong gluten-free diet. However, those with the skin condition known as dermatitis herpetiformis also need to eat gluten-free foods. While it is estimated that coeliac disease affects 1 in every 250 Australians, dermatitis herpetiformis is much rarer and is seen mostly in people who also have coeliac disease. Other people avoid wheat because they have an allergic reaction to it. Wheat allergy is quite rare and typically occurs only in children. There are also people who have none of the above medical conditions and yet become quite uncomfortable when they eat wheat. This is generally classified as wheat or gluten intolerance and the avoidance of gluten products tends to be less strict.

Living with food restrictions requires vigilance and patience from those who suffer the consequences of eating the wrong food, as well as from their family and friends. A person who suffers from coeliac disease cannot eat a grain protein known as gluten. Gluten is found in large amounts in wheat, triticale, rye and barley, and to a much lesser degree in oats. Ingredients derived from these grains, including wheat starch, malt and some thickeners, contain sufficient quantities of gluten to cause symptoms in some people with coeliac disease.

Avoiding gluten in every mouthful of food, drink and medication requires an awareness of ingredients used and an understanding of what to look for when reading a food label. It can be difficult to purchase gluten-free snacks, school lunches or fast takeaway foods, or to order food in restaurants, because not all food staff know where gluten can be found, especially the very small amounts. Even a simple dinner with friends, a child's birthday party or a visit to a friend's home after school requires food planning for anyone who needs to avoid gluten.

This book is the key to helping you solve some of the questions about where gluten is found and it also contains many delicious recipes for different occasions. It is useful not only for those avoiding gluten, but also for their friends and relatives who need to prepare and serve gluten-free foods.

## main sources of gluten

- ◆ **wheat** including atta, bran, bulgur, durum, kamut, semolina, spelt, wheatgerm
- ◆ **triticale** – a hybrid of wheat and rye
- ◆ **rye**
- ◆ **barley**

## minor sources of gluten

- ◆ **malt**
- ◆ **oats**
- ◆ **wheat starch** including wheaten cornflour

## coeliac disease

Coeliac disease is believed to be one of the most common gastrointestinal diseases found in Caucasians today. It can develop in infancy, childhood or at any time during adulthood. It appears to affect more women than men, and tends to be hereditary.

When gluten is eaten by a person with coeliac disease, a series of reactions occur in the gut that damage and flatten the lining of the small intestine. The lining is usually made up of small finger-like ridges, called villi, which help the body absorb the nutrients from the food eaten. The flattening of the villi is called villous atrophy. When this occurs, less of the food eaten can be absorbed into the body. Coeliac disease is treated by following a lifelong gluten-free diet.

### symptoms

Symptoms can vary depending on age, sensitivity to gluten, and degree of impairment of nutrient absorption. Traditionally the most common symptoms are weight loss or failure to thrive in young babies, diarrhoea, reflux, abdominal cramping, bloating, flatulence, nausea, vomiting, muscle wasting, and malabsorption of virtually all nutrients.

Today many adults and children do not present with these severe signs of coeliac disease, dominated by gastrointestinal complaints. It is quite a challenge for doctors to diagnose, since constipation, headaches, sub-optimal school performance, mild gut upsets, low blood iron, fatigue, multiple miscarriages, osteoporosis, bone fractures or general malaise may be the only clues to suggest the presence of the disease.

## diagnosis

Although there are a number of blood tests to screen for coeliac disease, only a small bowel biopsy can diagnose the condition. If you suspect you have coeliac disease, consult your doctor before making any dietary changes. Do not experiment with a gluten-free diet as you must be regularly eating foods that contain gluten when the blood tests and small bowel biopsy are carried out.

## associated conditions

The number of people being diagnosed with coeliac disease has increased in the last five to ten years because the blood tests allow people to be screened more easily. As a result, people with mild symptoms and even some who appear to have no symptoms at all are currently being diagnosed with coeliac disease. Those with insulin-dependent diabetes, thyroid disease or osteoporosis have been found to be more likely to have coeliac disease than others in the population. It has been noted that in some people insulin and thyroid medications are better absorbed, and often the doses can be reduced after following a gluten-free diet for some time.

## gluten-free diet

Even those with few or no symptoms are required to follow a lifelong gluten-free diet in order to avoid long-term complications of coeliac disease. Sufferers of the disease have an increased risk of developing a cancer somewhere in the gastrointestinal tract, but the chance of this decreases after following a gluten-free diet for five years. The avoidance of gluten will also lead to the regrowth of the villi in the small intestine so any nutrient deficiency can be corrected. These nutrient deficiencies commonly include low blood iron and folate, which could cause anaemia and fatigue, and diminished calcium absorption, which could cause a weakening of the bones, resulting in bone fractures or osteoporosis.

## gluten-free foods

Fresh milk, butter, cheese, fruit, vegetables, legumes, seeds, red meat, chicken and seafood are all gluten free. Tea, coffee and wine can be consumed, but regular beers must be excluded. Refer to the list below for gluten-free flours and grains.

## dermatitis herpetiformis

Dermatitis herpetiformis (DH) is a gluten-sensitive, blistering skin disease. Found more often in males, these small, intensely itchy blisters are usually located around the elbows, knees and buttocks. Many people with DH have few gastrointestinal symptoms, even though they also have coeliac disease. A skin biopsy of the blistered area is necessary to diagnose DH. Medication is usually given to control the rash in the short term. However, a gluten-free diet is recommended for lifelong control of the rash.

## wheat allergy

Wheat allergy is usually seen in young children. It is generally mild and most children grow out of it quite quickly. True food allergy tends to arise in families who have a history of childhood eczema or asthma. It occurs when the body produces an antibody to the wheat protein. Most children eventually stop producing this antibody.

## gluten-free flours, grains & alternatives

- amaranth
- arrowroot
- buckwheat
- carob
- corn (maize) including maize cornflour (cornstarch)
- guar gum
- legume flours including chickpea flour (besan)
- lentil flour
- lupin
- millet
- nut flours including almond and hazelnut meal
- polenta (cornmeal)
- potato flour (starch)
- psyllium
- quinoa
- rapeseed
- rice including rice bran, rice flour
- sago
- seeds including linseeds (flaxseeds), pepitas (pumpkin seeds), poppy seeds, sesame seeds
- sorghum
- soy flour
- tapioca
- xanthan gum

The majority of wheat allergies are mild. The symptoms may include itchy skin, eczema, or cold- or flu-like symptoms. In the rare case of a severe allergy, symptoms such as swelling and itchiness of the tongue and mouth, stomach cramps, vomiting or diarrhoea may occur within minutes of any wheat contacting the mouth. In extremely rare cases, wheat has been known to cause anaphylaxis, or difficulty in breathing, in children or adults if they have eaten wheat around the same time that they have done intense exercise. In this case, adrenaline needs to be administered immediately.

A simple skin prick test or blood test by a doctor can confirm whether or not an allergy to wheat is present. If a severe allergy is present, wheat must be strictly avoided, but other gluten grains can usually be eaten. If a very mild allergy is present, some people are able to eat a small amount of wheat, depending on the symptoms experienced. Let your healthcare team guide you on the exclusion of wheat from the diet.

## food intolerance

An intolerance to wheat can mimic many of the symptoms of coeliac disease, yet if a biopsy of the small bowel shows that the gut is normal, coeliac disease is not present. Many people are able to reduce their symptoms of intolerance by decreasing the amount of wheat and/or gluten in an otherwise balanced and varied diet, without the need for total wheat exclusion.

Food intolerances usually have more than one trigger. Other possible triggers include food additives (preservatives and colours), natural food chemicals (salicylates, amines and glutamates) and lactose or fructose malabsorption. Consult a doctor or dietitian who specialises in food intolerances for investigation.

## nutritional issues

If you suffer from coeliac disease, it is not unusual to gain weight when you start a gluten-free diet because the body is beginning to fully absorb its food. The first priority when starting the diet is to familiarise yourself with the foods you can have. Once you are feeling more comfortable, you can address any weight issues that arise. Some people welcome the weight gain, but others do not. Some find that being unable to eat gluten-containing snacks means that they snack less,

and this helps to maintain their weight. Others may need to become aware of the amount of fats and oils contained in food, the portion size of the food they eat and the amount of exercise that they are doing.

## fibre

As with all diets, if a variety of foods are eaten from each of the food groups, the diet will be nutritionally adequate. Grains supply the body with the B-group vitamins, fibre and carbohydrate. The B vitamins and carbohydrate are still adequately supplied when eating gluten-free grains, but the fibre levels are reduced. Maize cornflour, white rice flour and potato flour are the most frequently used flours in commercial gluten-free breads, pastas and snacks. The husk or fibrous skin is not present in the flour, so these products can be very low in fibre compared to the equivalent gluten-containing products.

The foods listed below are good sources of fibre to include in your diet and cooking. As well as containing fibre, many of these foods provide vitamins and minerals that are required for good health.

### high-fibre products

- brown rice
- brown rice flour
- buckwheat flour
- buckwheat grits
- chickpea flour (besan)
- dried fruit
- fresh fruit – including the skin
- high-fibre supplements – rice bran, amaranth or psyllium husks
- Hi-maize flour
- legumes or beans – add to extend casseroles
- lentils or split peas – add to soups and casseroles
- nuts – not recommended for children under five years
- parboiled white rice
- seeds – add to breakfast cereals and baking
- soybeans
- soy flour
- soy grits
- vegetables – including the skin

## calcium

When the villi are damaged, the production of the enzyme lactase is reduced. Therefore the gut loses some of its ability to break down the lactose sugar in dairy products. Many people with mild symptoms have been told that they have lactose intolerance and have avoided dairy products without taking supplementary calcium. In addition, calcium absorption is often decreased when the villi are damaged. This lack of both dietary and absorbed calcium can lead to impaired bone mineralisation, resulting in bones that may break more easily. This is referred to as osteopenia or, when severe, osteoporosis. Ensuring adequate calcium intake is very important. Dairy foods are the best source of calcium. Choose three serves of dairy foods each day from milk, cheese or yoghurt. Other non-dairy calcium sources include fortified soy or rice milk, nuts, seeds, and fish with edible bones. If the villi do not return to normal, some people may require calcium and vitamin D supplements. Consult your healthcare team before taking any supplements.

### iron and folate

Iron and folate deficiencies are often found on diagnosis of coeliac disease. Folate intake is often low in a gluten-free diet. Unlike gluten-containing breads and breakfast cereals, very few commercial gluten-free products are fortified with extra nutrients. The best sources of iron are red and white meat and fish, followed by eggs, legumes and nuts. The iron found in vegetables is not easily absorbed by the body. The absorption of iron is enhanced if foods containing vitamin C, such as cabbage, capsicum (bell pepper), tomato or citrus fruits, are eaten at the same time. Folate can be found naturally in liver, cabbage, spinach, peanuts, peas and oranges.

Occasionally iron and/or folate supplements may be necessary for people on a gluten-free diet. Consult your healthcare team before taking any supplements.

## understanding the gluten content of foods

When trying to either reduce or avoid gluten in the diet, it is important to understand that not all foods contain equal amounts of gluten. Grains and flours derived from wheat, triticale, rye and barley will include the whole protein fraction of the grain, which is where the gluten is found. The following table lists many of the foods that use flours ground from these grains as major ingredients, and therefore contain large quantities of gluten.

Regular beer, malt and oats contain less gluten protein than the above grains. Because it is hard to measure their gluten content accurately, most health professionals in Australia recommend that they are avoided in a gluten-free diet.

### products containing large quantities of gluten

- bagels
- biscuits
- bread – white, wholegrain, wholemeal, lavash, pita
- breadcrumbs
- breakfast cereals made using wheat
- cakes
- couscous
- crackers
- crumpets
- muesli
- muesli bars
- muffins
- noodles – wheat, egg
- pasta
- pastry
- pearl barley
- pies
- pizza
- semolina
- wheat bran
- wheat flour – plain, self-raising
- wheatgerm
- wheatmeal

When wheat flour is washed with water, the protein fraction is separated from the starch fraction. The starch is further refined to form many ingredients that can contain residual gluten, roughly less than 200 parts per million. The more refined the ingredient, the less gluten is detected. Such ingredients can be found in the table below. Many people who suffer from a wheat and/or gluten intolerance can eat these foods. However, the recipes in this book exclude all of these uncertain ingredients.

### ingredients containing small amounts of detectable gluten

- beverage whitener – maltodextrin (wheat)
- dextrin (wheat)
- malt extract (barley)
- malt vinegar
- maltodextrin (wheat)
- modified starch (wheat)
- thickeners – numbers 1400–1450 (wheat)
- soy sauce (wheat)
- starch (wheat)
- wheaten cornflour (wheat)

There are also some highly refined foods that are derived from wheat but contain no detectable gluten, using the best detection methods currently available. Any product labelled as 'gluten free' in Australia must not contain any detectable gluten, any oats or malt, or any ingredient derived from these two grains.

Currently the tests used by manufacturers detect as little as 5–20 parts per million of gluten. If gluten does exist in foods at levels less than this, research studies have not been able to prove that these levels are harmful for most people with coeliac disease, and the product is therefore labelled as being 'gluten free'. Ingredients that are refined from wheat, yet contain no detectable gluten, are shown in the table below. The vast majority of people with coeliac disease can eat these ingredients.

## products made from wheat that contain no detectable gluten

- caramel colour (wheat)
- dextrose (wheat)
- glucose powder (wheat)
- glucose syrup (wheat)

## food labels

In Australia and New Zealand, foods can be labelled either 'gluten free' or 'low gluten'. The 'gluten-free' food standard is defined above. Seen less frequently, a 'low gluten' food is permitted to contain ingredients such as wheat starch, malt or oats, as long as the total gluten detected is no more than 200 parts per million.

In December 2004 it became compulsory in Australia for manufacturers to print, in the 'Ingredients' section of all product labels, whether the ingredients used have been derived from a gluten-containing grain. This is most often written in the format: starch (wheat); malt (barley).

Ingredients such as beverage whitener or curry powder are called compound ingredients because they are composed of two or more ingredients. Under the new law, any part of a compound ingredient that has come from a gluten-containing grain must be declared on the label; for example: beverage whitener (maltodextrin [wheat]).

Ingredients that are derived from gluten and are used in the process of making a product, such as flour coatings on confectionery moulds, are called processing aids. The use of these must be stated on the label, but not necessarily under the list of ingredients; for example: moulding starch (wheat).

Sometimes ingredients, such as thickeners (numbers 1400–1450) or starches, can be derived from corn (maize), tapioca, potato or wheat. In this case, the manufacturer only has to label the ingredient if it has been derived from wheat, the gluten-containing grain; for example: starch (wheat); 1442 (wheat). If the ingredient has been derived from corn, the manufacturer does not have to state this; for example: starch; 1442.

Under this new system, if an ingredient does not state that it has been derived from a gluten-containing grain, such as wheat, then by default it generally indicates that it has been derived from a gluten-free grain, such as corn. Sometimes a summary statement is included instead, to indicate that an ingredient from a gluten source was used. Remember that if you see 'glucose syrup (wheat)' it is considered to be gluten free as it contains no detectable gluten.

## medication labels

It is essential to check that all medications and supplements, whether prescribed by a doctor or purchased over the counter, are gluten free. Although these rarely contain flour as such, they may contain starches that have been derived from wheat. Most often these are wheat starch or pre-gel starch (wheat).

Medications and supplements usually list only their drug, vitamin or mineral components. They are not required by law to list all the 'filler' ingredients used to make up the whole tablet. However, if a 'filler' is derived from a gluten-containing grain it must be defined on the label. Ask your doctor or pharmacist to refer to a reference guide to see if your medication or supplement has been listed as gluten free.

Since July 2004, the pharmaceutical labelling regulations in Australia have had to mirror the food standard regulations with respect to ingredients that can be called gluten free. If in doubt, check with the manufacturer yourself. Be aware that similar products produced by different manufacturers may contain different 'filler' ingredients. Each individual medication or supplement needs to be checked for gluten content.

# eating out

Eating out can become difficult and tedious. Try to frequent the same restaurants in your area so that they get to know you, and you get to know their menu and what choices are available to you. Your local coeliac society can often provide you with a list of restaurants that are recommended by other members as being helpful and supportive of gluten-free diets. The Coeliac Society of Australia supplies each member with a card that can be presented to food staff, summarising the main ingredients that should be avoided. See page 128 for contact details.

If you are self conscious about having a lengthy discussion concerning the menu in front of friends or work colleagues, try to contact the restaurant beforehand to discuss the choices and make your meal selection.

When accepting invitations to large functions, it is very important to inform the organisers that you require a gluten-free diet. Inform the person waiting on your table that you have requested gluten-free food so they know who to give it to. If a mistake is made with your meal, politely return it and request the gluten-free version again.

## restaurant tips

1 Every meal should be discussed with the restaurant staff
2 All sauces and gravies need to be investigated (are the sauces made using flours or starches?)
3 All dressings need to be investigated (ask for wine, cider or balsamic vinegar, lemon or oil for salad dressings)
4 All marinades need to be investigated (have stocks, soy sauce or other sauces been used that may contain gluten?)
5 Avoid dumplings, pastries, battered and crumbed foods
6 Tacos, nachos and pappadams are usually gluten free
7 Some restaurants allow you to bring your own gluten-free pizza base or gluten-free pasta (ask them to boil the pasta in a fresh pan of water)
8 If you ask for your meat or seafood to be grilled, ensure that it has not been dusted in flour
9 Most desserts contain gluten
10 Ice cream, gelato, mousse, crème caramel, fruit salad and fruit compotes are generally acceptable
11 Check whether wheaten cornflour has been used in pavlovas or meringues

## takeaway food tips

1 Sandwich shops — take your own gluten-free bread, bread roll, taco, focaccia, rice or corn cake and ask them to fill it
2 Salads — enquire about the ingredients in the dressings or avoid them
3 Sushi bars — take your own gluten-free tamari to use instead of soy sauce; avoid battered or crumbed fillings
4 Baked jacket potatoes — choose gluten-free fillings
5 Nachos and tacos — most are suitable
6 Barbecue chicken — avoid skin or seasoning
7 Grilled or fried fish — avoid flour coating
8 Hot chips — check they are not dusted or coated with flour
9 Hamburger chains — take your own gluten-free bread roll and use their burger patty, tomato sauce, cheese slice, tomato, lettuce and beetroot
10 Ice creams — many are suitable, but avoid cones and wafers
11 Milkshakes — choose fresh fruit flavours as syrup flavours may contain gluten

Many people with coeliac disease have concerns that eating hot chips cooked in the same oil as other battered foods will contaminate the chips with gluten. This has never been proven. The oil used to cook chips is at a very high temperature, which could break down the gluten protein if any is present. Many people with coeliac disease eat hot chips, but some request the oil to be scooped clean before they're cooked.

## school lunch box ideas

Always check the ingredients of packaged and processed foods, as ingredients may vary between manufacturers.

- baked beans
- boiled eggs
- canned spaghetti – gluten free
- cold pizzas – gluten free
- corn cakes with suitable spreads
- corn cobs
- corn, rice or vegetable pasta salads
- corn tortillas with meat and salad fillings
- focaccias – gluten free, with meat and salad fillings

- fried rice – use gluten-free tamari rather than soy sauce
- hamburgers – use gluten-free rolls
- pancakes – gluten free, wrapped around sweet or savoury fillings
- potato salads
- quiches – use gluten-free pastry
- rice cakes with suitable toppings
- rice noodle salads
- rice salads
- sandwiches – use gluten-free bread
- sausage rolls – use gluten-free pastry
- soup – gluten free, with rice crackers
- unprocessed cold meat, salad and rice crackers

## snack ideas

Always check the ingredients of packaged and processed foods, as ingredients may vary between manufacturers.

- canned fruit snacks
- corn chips and dip
- flavoured milk – avoid malt
- fruit – fresh, dried, frozen
- fruit sticks or fruit straps
- gluten-free biscuits, cakes, muffins, pikelets or scones

- gluten-free breakfast cereal snacks
- gluten-free custard snack packs
- gluten-free toasted bread or fruit bread
- ice blocks
- nuts – dry roasted may contain flour
- popcorn
- potato chips
- rice crackers and dip
- rice or corn crackers
- yoghurt

## celebrations

If you are hosting a celebration, it is easy to ensure that the food served is gluten free. However, if you are a guest at a celebration, you may need to make some delicate negotiations before the event. It is best to give the hosts plenty of prior notice so they can take your dietary requirements into account when deciding on the menu. Close friends are usually aware of your needs and you can help by supplying them with recipes, or you can offer to bring a gluten-free dish.

Some shops make or stock gluten-free hot cross buns, Christmas cakes, puddings and other celebration food at the appropriate time of year. Your local coeliac society can often advise you on where to purchase these products, or you can bake them yourself. Some commercial cake shops also sell gluten-free cakes.

Birthday parties can be difficult for children who need to avoid wheat and gluten. You may like to talk to the parents hosting the party to see what food they are planning to serve and if you can send some gluten-free alternatives with your child. Lollies and chocolates taken home from the party may not be appropriate, so you may wish to supply acceptable ones yourself. When you are hosting your child's birthday party, remember that the other children are not used to eating gluten-free products, so choose an ice cream cake (page 92) or pavlova-based cake (page 67).

Kim Faulkner-Hogg, PhD, Dietitian

## children's party food

Always check the ingredients of packaged and processed foods, as ingredients may vary between manufacturers.

- cocktail frankfurts – gluten free
- corn chips
- frozen chocolate-coated bananas
- fruit – fresh, dried, frozen
- ham off the bone and cheese slices

- hot potato wedges – not flour coated
- pizza squares – gluten free
- popcorn – plain or coloured
- potato chips
- rainbow jelly cups
- rice puff chocolate crackles
- rice snacks and dips
- sausage rolls – use gluten-free pastry
- soft drinks, fruit juice

# gluten-free replacements for bread

rice cakes

inari tofu

corn cakes

pan fried tofu

nori seaweed sheets

gluten-free bread

taco shells

buckwheat crispbread

white corn tortillas

lettuce leaves

omelette

rice paper rounds

baby rice cereal

gluten-free cornflour

shredded & desiccated coconut

gluten-free flour

gluten-free baking powder

gluten-free bread mix

dried yeast

amaranth flour & chickpea flour (besan)

hazelnut meal & almond meal

xanthan gum

gluten-free custard powder

rice flour & brown rice flour

WARD'S
baking
powder
GLUTEN FREE
125g NET

# breakfast

sweet quinoa fruit compote

## sweet quinoa fruit compote  serves 4

200 g (6¹/2 oz) dried
  pears, roughly
  chopped
100 g (3¹/3 oz) dried
  apricots, roughly
  chopped
100 g (3¹/3 oz) pitted
  dates, roughly
  chopped
100 g (3¹/3 oz) raisins

3 cups (750 ml/24 fl oz)
  unsweetened apple
  juice
1 teaspoon orange-
  flower water
1 cinnamon stick
¹/2 cup (85 g/2³/4 oz)
  quinoa
1¹/2 cups (375 ml/
  12 fl oz) water

**1** Put the pears, apricots, dates and raisins into a bowl and mix to combine.

**2** Put the apple juice, orange-flower water and cinnamon stick into a pan and bring to the boil.

**3** Add the quinoa, dried fruit mixture and water to the pan and simmer for 30 minutes or until the quinoa is soft and translucent. Serve hot or cold with gluten-free vanilla yoghurt.

**per serve** fat 1.8 g ▌ saturated fat 0.2 g ▌ protein 5.5 g ▌ carbohydrate 109.2 g ▌ fibre 12.2 g ▌ cholesterol 0 mg ▌ sodium 55 mg ▌ energy 2036 kJ (486 Cal) ▌ gi low ▼

## family berry pancake  serves 6–8

canola oil spray
1¹/2 cups (170 g/5²/3 oz)
  gluten-free self-raising
  flour
1 teaspoon xanthan gum
2 tablespoons caster
  sugar
2 eggs, lightly beaten

60 g (2 oz) butter,
  melted
300 ml (10 fl oz) milk
200 g (6¹/2 oz) mixed
  berries
2 tablespoons pure
  maple syrup

**1** Preheat oven to 180°C (350°F/Gas 4). Lightly spray the base and side of a 22 cm (9 in) non-stick ovenproof fry pan with canola oil spray.

**2** Sift the flour and xanthan gum into a bowl and stir in the sugar. Make a well in the centre.

**3** Whisk together the eggs, butter and milk. Pour into the well and stir until smooth.

**4** Heat the fry pan over medium heat. Add the pancake mixture and cook for 3–5 minutes or until the base is golden.

**5** Press the berries into the top of the pancake and transfer to the oven. Bake for 30–40 minutes or until risen and golden.

**6** Drizzle the pancake with the maple syrup and serve in wedges from the pan, topped with a little gluten-free vanilla yoghurt.

**per serve (8)** fat 9.4 g ▌ saturated fat 5.5 g ▌ protein 3.5 g ▌ carbohydrate 25 g ▌ fibre 1 g ▌ cholesterol 71 mg ▌ sodium 65 mg ▌ energy 825 kJ (197 Cal) ▌ gi low–med ▼–◆

▌ Replace the butter with reduced-fat margarine if you want to lower the fat and calorie content.

family berry pancake

**soy grit cakes with smoked salmon**

**black sticky rice with tropical fruit**

## soy grit cakes with smoked salmon  serves 6

5 cups (1.25 litres/
  40 fl oz) water
1 cup (190 g/6$^{1}/_{4}$ oz)
  coarse dry soy grits
20 g ($^{3}/_{4}$ oz) reduced-fat
  margarine
4 eggs, lightly beaten
$^{1}/_{3}$ cup (40 g/1$^{1}/_{3}$ oz)
  grated reduced-fat
  cheddar cheese
2 tablespoons chopped
  fresh herbs (dill,
  parsley, basil)

2 tablespoons chopped
  capers
50 g (1$^{2}/_{3}$ oz) rocket
  (arugula)
2 tablespoons light sour
  cream
100 g (3$^{1}/_{3}$ oz) smoked
  salmon
12 caperberries, halved
cracked black pepper

**1** Preheat oven to 180°C (350°F/Gas 4). Lightly grease a 20 cm (8 in) square cake tin and line with baking paper.
**2** Pour the water into a pan and bring to the boil. Slowly add the soy grits, whisking constantly. Reduce the heat and simmer for 30 minutes or until soft.
**3** Remove from the heat and stir in the margarine, eggs, cheese, herbs and capers. Pour into the prepared tin and bake for 30 minutes or until set. Cool slightly, then cut into 6 cakes.
**4** Top each cake with some rocket, sour cream, a few slices of smoked salmon and the caperberries. Sprinkle with cracked black pepper.

**per serve**  fat 18 g ▌ saturated fat 3.9 g ▌ protein 32 g ▌ carbohydrate 5.9 g ▌ fibre 3.4 g ▌ cholesterol 141 mg ▌ sodium 443 mg ▌ energy 1308 kJ (312 Cal) ▌ gi low ▼

▌Use omega-3 enriched eggs to add more healthy omega-3 fat to this dish.

## black sticky rice with tropical fruit  serves 4

1 cup (200 g/6$^{1}/_{2}$ oz)
  black rice
2 cups (500 ml/16 fl oz)
  water
1 cup (250 ml/8 fl oz)
  reduced-fat coconut
  milk

$^{1}/_{4}$ cup (60 g/2 oz)
  grated palm sugar
  or brown sugar
1 mango, sliced
1 small red papaya,
  sliced
2 passionfruit

**1** Put the rice into a bowl, cover with water and set aside to soak overnight. Drain the rice.
**2** Transfer the rice to a medium pan with the water. Bring to the boil, stirring frequently, then reduce the heat and cook at a low boil for 20 minutes or until the rice is soft. Drain well.
**3** Heat the coconut milk and sugar in a separate pan and stir until the sugar has dissolved. Add the drained rice and cook over low heat for 5 minutes. Remove the pan from the heat, cover and set aside for 15 minutes.
**4** Divide the sticky rice among 4 bowls and top with the mango, papaya and passionfruit.

**per serve**  fat 4.2 g ▌ saturated fat 2.8 g ▌ protein 4.1 g ▌ carbohydrate 66.7 g ▌ fibre 4.8 g ▌ cholesterol 0 mg ▌ sodium 27 mg ▌ energy 1300 kJ (310 Cal) ▌ gi med–high ◆–▲

▌You can also cook the soaked rice with the water, coconut milk and palm sugar in a rice cooker.

breakfast

cherry & blueberry polenta

## mini breakfast quiches   serves 4

4 gluten-free white corn
  tortillas
1 egg white
1/3 cup (35 g/1 oz) finely
  grated parmesan
  cheese
2 eggs, lightly beaten
1/2 cup (125 ml/4 fl oz)
  reduced-fat milk
salt and pepper

100 g (3 1/3 oz) gluten-
  free 97% fat-free ham,
  chopped
2 spring onions
  (scallions), sliced
100 g (3 1/3 oz) cherry
  tomatoes, halved
1 tablespoon chopped
  fresh basil

## cherry & blueberry polenta   serves 6

4 cups (1 litre/32 fl oz)
  gluten-free soy milk
1 cup (150 g/5 oz) fine
  polenta (cornmeal)
2 tablespoons caster
  sugar
150 g (5 oz) blueberries

2 tablespoons cherry
  pure fruit spread
200 g (6 1/2 oz) gluten-
  free Greek-style plain
  yoghurt
1 tablespoon lemon
  myrtle honey

**1** Heat the soy milk in a pan over medium heat until almost boiling. Add the polenta in a fine, steady stream, whisking until combined.
**2** Using a wooden spoon, stir in the sugar and blueberries. Cook, stirring constantly, for 5 minutes or until the polenta is thick and creamy.
**3** Remove from the heat and swirl through the fruit spread. Cover and set aside for 5 minutes.
**4** Put the yoghurt into a bowl and gently swirl through the honey.
**5** Divide the polenta among 6 bowls and serve with the honeyed yoghurt.

**per serve** fat 8.9 g ▌ saturated fat 2.3 g ▌ protein 10.1 g ▌ carbohydrate 43.9 g ▌ fibre 2.1 g ▌ cholesterol 9 mg ▌ sodium 92 mg ▌ energy 1234 kJ (295 Cal) ▌ gi low ▼

**1** Preheat oven to 200°C (400°F/Gas 6). Line 4 x 1 cup (250 ml/8 fl oz) capacity muffin holes with baking paper.
**2** Lightly brush both sides of the corn tortillas with the egg white and carefully fit them into the muffin holes. Sprinkle any gaps with a little of the parmesan and bake for 15 minutes or until the tortillas are crisp and golden.
**3** Whisk together the eggs and milk and season with salt and pepper. Heat a non-stick fry pan over medium heat. Add the egg mixture to the pan and cook until it just starts to set, then stir until the mixture is lightly scrambled. Cook for 2 minutes.
**4** Divide the scrambled egg among the tortillas. Top with the ham, spring onions, tomatoes and basil and sprinkle with the remaining parmesan. Bake for 10 minutes or until the parmesan has melted.

**per serve** fat 7.5 g ▌ saturated fat 3.3 g ▌ protein 15.3 g ▌ carbohydrate 15.1 g ▌ fibre 2.2 g ▌ cholesterol 117 mg ▌ sodium 635 mg ▌ energy 811 kJ (194 Cal) ▌ gi low–med ▼–◆

▌ Use omega-3 enriched eggs and omega-3 enriched milk to add some healthy omega-3 fat to this dish.

mini breakfast quiches

spicy bacon quesadillas

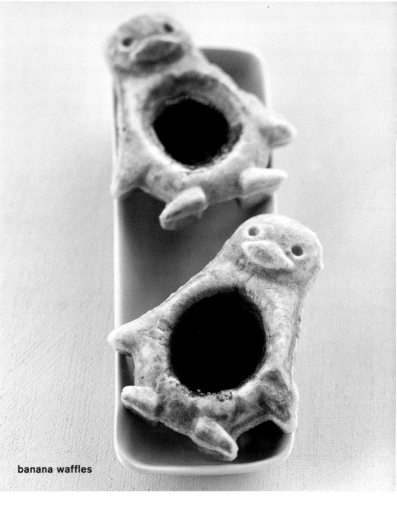

banana waffles

## spicy bacon quesadillas  serves 4

200 g (6¹/₂ oz) gluten-
free 97% fat-free
bacon
130 g (4¹/₂ oz) canned
corn kernels
1 tablespoon chopped
bottled jalapeños

1 cup (125 g/4 oz)
grated reduced-fat
cheddar cheese
2 tablespoons fresh
coriander (cilantro),
chopped
8 gluten-free white
corn tortillas

**1** Cook the bacon under a grill preheated to high
until crisp and golden brown. Cool slightly, then
roughly chop.
**2** Combine the bacon, corn, jalapeños, cheese and
coriander in a bowl.
**3** Place a tortilla in a non-stick fry pan and spread
with a quarter of the bacon mixture. Top with another
tortilla and weigh it down with a plate. Cook over
medium heat for 3 minutes or until the bottom tortilla
is crisp and golden.
**4** Slide the tortilla out of the pan and onto a plate.
Return to the pan and cook the other side until the
cheese is melted. Repeat with the remaining tortillas
and bacon mixture. Cut into wedges to serve.

**per serve** fat 8.2 g ▮ saturated fat 4 g ▮ protein 24.7 g
▮ carbohydrate 31.8 g ▮ fibre 4.3 g ▮ cholesterol 31 mg ▮ sodium
1261 mg ▮ energy 1266 kJ (302 Cal) ▮ gi low–med ▽–◆

## banana waffles  serves 6–8

2¹/₂ cups (300 g/10 oz)
gluten-free plain flour
pre-mix
1 teaspoon gluten-free
baking powder
1 tablespoon caster
sugar

80 g (2²/₃ oz) reduced-
fat margarine, melted
3 eggs, lightly beaten
1¹/₂ cups (375 ml/
12 fl oz) milk
2 medium ripe bananas,
sliced

**1** Preheat a waffle maker.
**2** Sift the flour and baking powder into a bowl
and stir in the sugar. Make a well in the centre.
**3** Whisk together the margarine, eggs and milk.
Gradually pour into the well and whisk until just
combined; the batter should still be lumpy.
**4** Spoon 1–2 tablespoons of the batter into the
waffle maker and place a few slices of banana in
the centre of the waffle. Cook until golden brown.
Keep warm while you cook the remaining batter.
Serve with pure maple syrup.

**per serve (8)** fat 9.9 g ▮ saturated fat 2.7 g ▮ protein 4.7 g
▮ carbohydrate 33.8 g ▮ fibre 1.2 g ▮ cholesterol 77 mg ▮ sodium
148 mg ▮ energy 1014 kJ (242 Cal) ▮ gi med ◆

hazelnut rice porridge

## baked ricotta with smoky beans serves 4

olive oil spray
cracked black pepper
350 g (12 oz) low-fat
  ricotta cheese
1 tablespoon olive oil
1 medium onion, finely
  chopped
1 teaspoon smoked
  paprika
400 g (13 oz) can butter
  beans, rinsed and
  drained

400 g (13 oz) can
  chopped tomatoes
1/4 cup (60 ml/2 fl oz)
  water
1 tablespoon brown
  sugar
2 teaspoons tomato
  paste
1 tablespoon chopped
  fresh parsley

**1** Preheat oven to 220°C (425°F/Gas 7). Spray 4 x
1/3 cup (80 ml/2$^2$/3 fl oz) capacity non-stick muffin
holes with olive oil spray and sprinkle with cracked
black pepper.
**2** Mash the ricotta and press into the muffin holes.
Bake for 30–40 minutes or until golden.
**3** Heat the oil in a large fry pan over medium heat.
Add the onion and paprika and cook for 5 minutes or
until the onion is soft and golden. Add the beans and
tomatoes and cook for 5 minutes.
**4** Combine the water, sugar and tomato paste and
stir until the sugar has dissolved. Add to the bean
mixture and cook for 10 minutes or until nearly all of
the liquid has been absorbed. Fold in the parsley.
**5** Serve the ricotta accompanied by the beans.
**per serve** fat 13.1 g ▮ saturated fat 5.7 g ▮ protein 11.8 g
▮ carbohydrate 11.3 g ▮ fibre 3.1 g ▮ cholesterol 37 mg ▮ sodium
248 mg ▮ energy 898 kJ (215 Cal) ▮ gi low ▽

## hazelnut rice porridge serves 4

4 cups (1 litre/32 fl oz)
  rice milk
2 cups (170 g/5$^2$/3 oz)
  gluten-free rice flakes
2 tablespoons brown
  sugar
1 teaspoon vanilla
  extract

1/4 cup (25 g/1 oz)
  hazelnut meal
4 sugar bananas, sliced
1 tablespoon caster
  sugar
1 teaspoon ground
  cinnamon

**1** Pour the rice milk into a pan and heat over
medium heat until almost boiling.
**2** Stir in the rice flakes, brown sugar, vanilla and
hazelnut meal. Cook, stirring, for 15 minutes or until
the porridge is thick and creamy.
**3** Arrange the sliced bananas on top of the porridge
and sprinkle with the combined caster sugar and
cinnamon. Serve with milk.
**per serve** fat 9.2 g ▮ saturated fat 1.4 g ▮ protein 8.6 g
▮ carbohydrate 106.5 g ▮ fibre 6.3 g ▮ cholesterol 0 mg ▮ sodium
127 mg ▮ energy 2337 kJ (558 Cal) ▮ gi high ▲

▮ Replace the rice milk with gluten-free soy milk, if
preferred. This will make the dish a low-GI meal.

baked ricotta with smoky beans

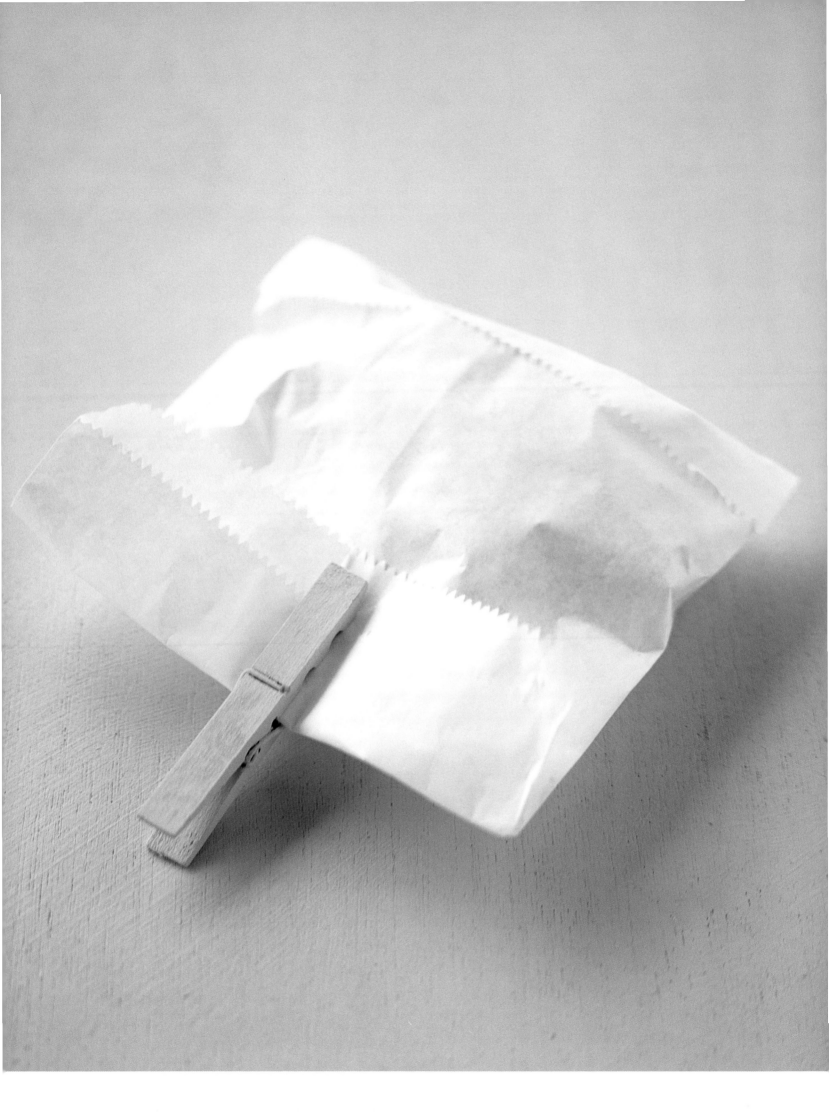

lunch

chicken pesto wraps

# lemon grass pork & noodle salad    serves 6

50 g (1²/₃ oz) mung
   bean (glass) noodles
300 g (10 oz) pork mince
2 cups (170 g/5²/₃ oz)
   finely grated carrot
2 cups (90 g/3 oz)
   shredded Chinese
   cabbage
¹/₂ cup (25 g/1 oz)
   shredded fresh mint
   leaves
¹/₂ cup (8 g/¹/₄ oz) fresh
   coriander (cilantro)
   leaves

50 g (1²/₃ oz) flaked
   almonds
1 large red chilli, seeded
   and cut into thin strips
2 tablespoons gluten-
   free tamari
2 tablespoons apple
   cider vinegar
2 teaspoons caster
   sugar
1 teaspoon sesame oil
1 tablespoon chopped
   lemon grass

**1**  Put the noodles into a bowl, cover with boiling water and set aside for 10 minutes or until soft. Drain well. Cut the noodles into short lengths using kitchen scissors.
**2**  Meanwhile, heat a non-stick fry pan over high heat. Add the pork and cook for 5 minutes or until browned. Remove and set aside to cool slightly.
**3**  Put the noodles, pork, carrot, cabbage, mint, coriander, almonds and chilli into a large bowl and gently mix to combine.
**4**  Whisk together the tamari, vinegar, sugar, sesame oil and lemon grass. Pour over the salad and gently toss to combine.

**per serve**  fat 9 g ▌ saturated fat 1.7 g ▌ protein 13 g
▌ carbohydrate 11.3 g ▌ fibre 2.4 g ▌ cholesterol 30 mg ▌ sodium
386 mg ▌ energy 767 kJ (183 Cal) ▌ gi low ▽

# chicken pesto wraps    serves 4

4 gluten-free white
   corn tortillas
4 tablespoons pesto
   sauce
100 g (3¹/₃ oz) low-fat
   ricotta cheese
2 medium tomatoes,
   sliced

2 cups (300 g/10 oz)
   shredded skinless
   unseasoned barbecue
   chicken
50 g (1²/₃ oz) baby
   English spinach

**1**  Preheat a sandwich press.
**2**  Lay the tortillas on a work surface. Combine the pesto and ricotta and spread over the tortillas.
**3**  Divide the tomatoes, chicken and spinach among the tortillas and roll up.
**4**  Cook the wraps in the sandwich press until crisp and golden. Cut in half and serve with salad.

**per serve**  fat 17.4 g ▌ saturated fat 5 g ▌ protein 28 g
▌ carbohydrate 14.8 g ▌ fibre 3.3 g ▌ cholesterol 91 mg ▌ sodium
363 mg ▌ energy 1400 kJ (334 Cal) ▌ gi low ▽

lunch

lemon grass pork & noodle salad

thai salmon salad baskets

corn pasta salad

# thai salmon salad baskets serves 4

olive oil spray
4 rice paper rounds,
   23 cm (9 in) diameter
400 g (13 oz) salmon
   fillet
50 g (1²/₃ oz) Asian
   salad mix

1 medium Lebanese
   cucumber, thinly sliced
2 tablespoons fried
   Asian shallots
1 tablespoon gluten-free
   sweet chilli sauce
1 tablespoon fish sauce
1 tablespoon lime juice

**1** Preheat oven to 200°C (400°F/Gas 6). Spray
4 x 1 cup (250 ml/8 fl oz) capacity non-stick muffin
holes with olive oil spray.
**2** Soak one rice paper round at a time in water until
soft. Arrange one round in each muffin hole and
spray with olive oil spray. Bake for 15–20 minutes or
until crisp and golden. Set aside to cool completely
before removing the baskets from the muffin pan.
**3** Cook the salmon in a lightly oiled chargrill pan
until cooked to your liking. Cool slightly, then break
into bite-sized pieces.
**4** Put the salad mix, cucumber, fried shallots and
salmon into a bowl.
**5** Whisk together the sweet chilli sauce, fish sauce
and lime juice. Pour over the salad and gently toss
to combine. Divide the salad among the baskets and
serve immediately.

**per serve** fat 8.3 g ▮ saturated fat 1.8 g ▮ protein 21 g
▮ carbohydrate 10.9 g ▮ fibre 0.7 g ▮ cholesterol 52 mg ▮ sodium
694 mg ▮ energy 859 kJ (205 Cal) ▮ gi low ▼

# corn pasta salad serves 4

250 g (8 oz) gluten-free
   corn and rice pasta
200 g (6¹/₂ oz) chargrilled
   red capsicum (bell
   pepper), cut into thin
   strips
310 g (10 oz) can corn
   kernels, drained
200 g (6¹/₂ oz) artichoke
   hearts, chopped
50 g (1²/₃ oz) baby
   English spinach

1 tablespoon chopped
   fresh dill
1 tablespoon capers
1 tablespoon extra virgin
   olive oil
2 tablespoons apple
   cider vinegar
1 teaspoon gluten-free
   wholegrain mustard
1 teaspoon honey
2 hard-boiled eggs
cracked black pepper

**1** Cook the pasta in a large pan of rapidly boiling
water until just tender; do not overcook the pasta or
it will break up. Rinse under cold water and drain.
**2** Put the cooked pasta, capsicum, corn, artichokes,
spinach, dill and capers into a bowl and gently toss
to combine.
**3** Whisk together the olive oil, vinegar, mustard and
honey and pour over the salad. Grate the eggs over
the top and sprinkle with cracked black pepper.

**per serve** fat 9.2 g ▮ saturated fat 1.8 g ▮ protein 8.7 g
▮ carbohydrate 28.5 g ▮ fibre 7.1 g ▮ cholesterol 108 mg ▮ sodium
350 mg ▮ energy 1039 kJ (248 Cal) ▮ gi med ◆

**bean nachos**

## bacon, leek & ricotta slice serves 6–8

2 medium leeks, thinly
  sliced
1 tablespoon light olive
  oil
4 slices gluten-free 97%
  fat-free bacon, thinly
  sliced
6 eggs
1 cup (260 g/8¹/₃ oz)
  low-fat ricotta cheese

¹/₂ cup (125 ml/4 fl oz)
  light cream
¹/₂ cup (50 g/1²/₃ oz)
  grated parmesan
  cheese
1 tablespoon chopped
  fresh herbs (parsley,
  chives, sage)
salt and pepper

**1** Preheat oven to 180°C (350°F/Gas 4). Grease a 28 cm x 21 cm (11 in x 8¹/₂ in) ovenproof dish.
**2** Thoroughly rinse the sliced leeks and set aside to drain well.
**3** Heat the oil in a large fry pan over medium-high heat. Add the bacon and sauté until it starts to crisp. Add the leeks, toss well and sauté for 5–6 minutes or until the leeks are softened and lightly browned. Remove the pan from the heat.
**4** Lightly beat the eggs in a large bowl. Add the ricotta, cream, parmesan and herbs. Season with salt and pepper and mix to combine.
**5** Spread the bacon and leek mixture over the base of the prepared dish. Pour the egg mixture evenly over the top. Bake for 25–30 minutes or until firm.
**per serve (8)** fat 14.4 g ‖ saturated fat 6.8 g ‖ protein 13.7 g ‖ carbohydrate 2.5 g ‖ fibre 0.7 g ‖ cholesterol 173 mg ‖ sodium 411 mg ‖ energy 804 kJ (192 Cal) ‖ gi low ▼

## bean nachos serves 4

430 g (15 oz) can refried
  beans
400 g (13 oz) can mexe-
  beans, drained
1 medium avocado,
  mashed
1 tablespoon lime juice
salt and pepper
2 medium tomatoes,
  chopped

2 spring onions
  (scallions), sliced
1 tablespoon chopped
  fresh coriander
  (cilantro)
¹/₄ cup (65 g/2 oz)
  gluten-free Greek-style
  plain yoghurt
200 g (6¹/₂ oz) gluten-
  free low-fat baked
  corn chips

**1** Put the refried beans and mexe-beans into a pan. Cook over medium heat for 5 minutes or until heated through. Divide the beans among 4 bowls.
**2** Combine the avocado and lime juice and season with salt and pepper. Spoon on top of the beans.
**3** Put the tomatoes, spring onions and coriander into a bowl and mix to combine. Divide the tomato mixture among 4 bowls. Serve with the beans, yoghurt and corn chips.
**per serve** fat 17.9 g ‖ saturated fat 4.1 g ‖ protein 17.6 g ‖ carbohydrate 64.5 g ‖ fibre 14.2 g ‖ cholesterol 5 mg ‖ sodium 730 mg ‖ energy 2135 kJ (510 Cal) ‖ gi low–med ▼–◆

bacon, leek & ricotta slice

spinach & fetta pasta bake

**chunky potato, leek & quinoa soup**

## spinach & fetta pasta bake serves 6

8 cloves garlic, unpeeled
olive oil spray
100 g (3⅓ oz) baby
  English spinach
250 g (8 oz) gluten-free
  rice pasta shells
5 eggs
½ cup (125 ml/4 fl oz)
  light cream
2 spring onions
  (scallions), thinly sliced

½ cup (50 g/1⅔ oz)
  grated parmesan
  cheese
1 tablespoon finely
  chopped fresh herbs
  (thyme, chives,
  parsley)
100 g (3⅓ oz) soft
  Danish-style fetta
  cheese

**1** Preheat oven to 180°C (350°F/Gas 4). Lightly grease a 23 cm (9 in) ovenproof ceramic or glass pie dish.

**2** Place the garlic cloves on a baking tray and lightly spray with olive oil spray. Roast for 15 minutes or until the flesh has softened. Cool slightly, then squeeze the flesh out of the skins and finely chop.

**3** Wash the spinach and put into a pan. Cover and cook over medium heat for 5 minutes or until wilted. Cool, then squeeze out any moisture and finely chop.

**4** Cook the pasta shells in a large pan of rapidly boiling water until just tender; do not overcook the pasta or it will break up. Rinse under hot water and drain. Put the drained pasta and chopped spinach in the base of the prepared dish.

**5** Lightly beat the eggs in a large bowl. Add the cream, spring onions, parmesan, herbs and chopped garlic flesh and mix to combine. Pour over the pasta and spinach and crumble the fetta over the top. Bake for 25 minutes or until set.

**per serve** fat 15.6 g ▌ saturated fat 8.4 g ▌ protein 15.7 g ▌ carbohydrate 34.3 g ▌ fibre 2.4 g ▌ cholesterol 188 mg ▌ sodium 348 mg ▌ energy 1395 kJ (333 Cal) ▌ gi med–high ◆–▲

## chunky potato, leek & quinoa soup serves 4–6

1 tablespoon olive oil
2 medium leeks, thinly
  sliced
150 g (5 oz) gluten-free
  97% fat-free bacon,
  chopped
500 g (1 lb) potatoes,
  unpeeled, chopped
5 cups (1.25 litres/40 fl oz)
  gluten-free chicken or
  vegetable stock

salt and pepper
⅓ cup (60 g/2 oz)
  quinoa
400 g (13 oz) can
  cannellini beans,
  rinsed and drained
2 tablespoons snipped
  fresh chives

**1** Heat the oil in a large pan over medium heat. Add the sliced leeks and bacon and cook for 5 minutes or until the leeks are soft and golden.

**2** Add the potatoes and cook until they start to soften. Stir in the stock and season with salt and pepper. Bring to the boil, then reduce the heat and simmer, covered, for 10 minutes.

**3** Add the quinoa and cannellini beans and cook, covered, for 25 minutes or until the potato is soft and the quinoa is translucent.

**4** Stir in the chives, season with salt and pepper and serve immediately.

**per serve (6)** fat 4.9 g ▌ saturated fat 1 g ▌ protein 15.5 g ▌ carbohydrate 27 g ▌ fibre 6 g ▌ cholesterol 12 mg ▌ sodium 960 mg ▌ energy 927 kJ (221 Cal) ▌ gi low–med ▼–◆

chicken & noodle patties

# pumpkin, rice & millet slice serves 6

| | |
|---|---|
| ¹/₂ cup (105 g/3¹/₂ oz) millet | 1 tablespoon toasted sesame seeds |
| ¹/₂ cup (100 g/3¹/₃ oz) long-grain brown rice | 1 tablespoon sunflower seeds |
| 4 cups (1 litre/32 fl oz) water | 50 g (1²/₃ oz) mizuna or mixed salad leaves |
| 400 g (13 oz) peeled pumpkin, cut into wedges | 1 medium red capsicum (bell pepper), thinly sliced |
| ¹/₄ cup (60 ml/2 fl oz) gluten-free tamari | 2 celery sticks, shredded |
| 1 tablespoon pepitas (pumpkin seeds) | 2 tablespoons rice wine vinegar |
| | 1 tablespoon tahini |
| | 1 teaspoon sesame oil |

**1** Preheat oven to 200°C (400°F/Gas 6). Line a 28 cm x 18 cm (11 in x 7 in) rectangular cake tin with baking paper.
**2** Heat a dry fry pan over medium heat. Add the millet and brown rice and cook for 5 minutes or until golden brown.
**3** Transfer the millet and rice into a pan, add the water and cook over medium heat until the millet and rice are soft and all the water has been absorbed.
**4** Meanwhile, put the pumpkin on a baking tray and bake for 40 minutes or until soft. Cool slightly, then mash until smooth.
**5** Put the pumpkin, millet, rice and 1 tablespoon of the tamari into a bowl and mix well to combine. Press into the prepared tin, sprinkle with the pepitas, sesame seeds and sunflower seeds and bake for 40 minutes or until set. Set aside for 10 minutes before cutting into 6 slices.
**6** Put the mizuna, capsicum and celery into a bowl. Whisk together the remaining tamari, vinegar, tahini and sesame oil. Pour over the salad and toss to combine. Serve the slice topped with the salad.

**per serve** fat 7.3 g ▌saturated fat 1.1 g ▌protein 8.1 g ▌carbohydrate 30.4 g ▌fibre 4.6 g ▌cholesterol 0 mg ▌sodium 522 mg ▌energy 962 kJ (230 Cal) ▌gi med ◆

# chicken & noodle patties serves 6

| | |
|---|---|
| 60 g (2 oz) mung bean (glass) noodles | 1 tablespoon sambal oelek |
| 500 g (1 lb) skinless chicken thigh fillets, trimmed and chopped | 1 teaspoon grated fresh ginger |
| ¹/₂ cup (8 g/¹/₄ oz) fresh coriander (cilantro) leaves, torn | 1 teaspoon fish sauce |
| | ¹/₂ teaspoon black pepper |
| 2 spring onions (scallions), sliced | ¹/₂ teaspoon ground cinnamon |
| 2 cloves garlic, chopped | ¹/₄ cup (60 ml/2 fl oz) peanut oil |
| 2 tablespoons potato flour, plus extra, to coat | ¹/₂ cup (125 ml/4 fl oz) gluten-free sweet chilli sauce |

**1** Put the noodles into a bowl, cover with boiling water and set aside for 10 minutes or until soft. Drain well. Cut the noodles into short lengths.
**2** Put the chicken, coriander, spring onions, garlic, potato flour, sambal oelek, ginger, fish sauce, pepper and cinnamon into a food processor and process until well combined. Transfer to a large bowl.
**3** Add the noodles and mix well. Shape the mixture into 6 flat patties and coat in the extra potato flour.
**4** Heat the oil in a fry pan over medium-high heat. Fry the patties for 5 minutes each side or until firm. Drain on absorbent paper. Serve with the chilli sauce.

**per serve** fat 14.2 g ▌saturated fat 4.1 g ▌protein 15.8 g ▌carbohydrate 23.7 g ▌fibre 1 g ▌cholesterol 71 mg ▌sodium 390 mg ▌energy 1208 kJ (288 Cal) ▌gi low ▼

pumpkin, rice & millet slice

# snacks

apricot dream balls

## apple date slice serves 12

1 cup (180 g/6 oz) pitted
  dates, chopped
1 cup (250 ml/8 fl oz)
  water
1$^1$/$_2$ cups (180 g/6 oz)
  gluten-free plain flour
  pre-mix
1 cup (60 g/2 oz)
  shredded coconut

1 cup (115 g/3$^2$/$_3$ oz)
  pecan halves, chopped
1 cup (250 ml/8 fl oz)
  rice milk
2 apples, peeled, cored
  and sliced
2 tablespoons cherry
  pure fruit spread

**1** Preheat oven to 180°C (350°F/Gas 4). Line a 30 cm x 20 cm (12 in x 8 in) rectangular cake tin with baking paper.
**2** Put the dates and water into a pan and bring to the boil. Cook over medium heat for 5 minutes or until most of the liquid has been absorbed.
**3** Transfer the date mixture to a bowl, add the flour, coconut, pecans and rice milk and mix to combine.
**4** Spoon the mixture into the prepared tin. Arrange the apple slices on top of the mixture and brush with the fruit spread. Bake for 40 minutes or until a skewer comes out clean when inserted into the centre.

**per serve**  fat 10.5 g ▮ saturated fat 3.4 g ▮ protein 2 g
▮ carbohydrate 27.9 g ▮ fibre 3.8 g ▮ cholesterol 0 mg ▮ sodium
16 mg ▮ energy 913 kJ (218 Cal) ▮ gi med ◆

## apricot dream balls makes 24

200 g (6$^1$/$_2$ oz) dried fruit
  medley
100 g (3$^1$/$_3$ oz) dried
  apricots

1 tablespoon reduced-fat
  coconut milk
$^1$/$_4$ cup (25 g/1 oz)
  desiccated coconut

**1** Put the fruit medley, apricots and coconut milk into a food processor and process until the mixture comes together.
**2** Shape tablespoons of the mixture into balls and roll in the desiccated coconut. Chill until firm.

**per ball**  fat 0.7 g ▮ saturated fat 0.6 g ▮ protein 0.5 g
▮ carbohydrate 7 g ▮ fibre 1.2 g ▮ cholesterol 0 mg ▮ sodium 4 mg
▮ energy 160 kJ (38 Cal) ▮ gi low ▽

apple date slice

apple & strawberry almond scones

tamari chips, nuts & seeds

## apple & strawberry almond scones  makes 9

2 cups (230 g/7¼ oz) gluten-free self-raising flour

½ cup (25 g/1 oz) baby rice cereal

½ cup (55 g/1²/₃ oz) almond meal

1 teaspoon xanthan gum

1 teaspoon gluten-free baking powder

1 teaspoon ground cinnamon

40 g (1⅓ oz) cold butter, chopped

1¼ cups (310 ml/ 10 fl oz) low-fat milk, plus extra, for brushing

140 g (4½ oz) apple and strawberry puree

**1** Preheat oven to 220°C (425°F/Gas 7). Line a baking tray with baking paper.

**2** Sift the flour, rice cereal, almond meal, xanthan gum, baking powder and cinnamon into a bowl, tip the husks into the bowl and mix to combine. Using your fingertips, rub the butter into the flour mixture until the mixture resembles fine breadcrumbs.

**3** Make a well in the centre and stir in the milk with a flat-bladed knife, using a cutting action, until the dough comes together in clumps. Gather the dough into a ball.

**4** Pat the dough out between 2 sheets of baking paper into a 2 cm (¾ in) thick square. Cut the dough into 9 scones. Use your thumb to make a deep indentation in each scone and fill with the apple and strawberry puree.

**5** Put the scones on the prepared tray, lightly brush with milk and bake for 15 minutes or until risen and golden brown.

**per scone**  fat 7.2 g ▮ saturated fat 2.7 g ▮ protein 3 g ▮ carbohydrate 22.7 g ▮ fibre 2 g ▮ cholesterol 12 mg ▮ sodium 106 mg ▮ energy 705 kJ (168 Cal) ▮ gi med ◆

## tamari chips, nuts & seeds  serves 10

200 g (6½ oz) chickpea chips

100 g (3⅓ oz) raw almonds

2 tablespoons pepitas (pumpkin seeds)

1 tablespoon gluten-free tamari

2 teaspoons gluten-free sweet chilli sauce

**1** Preheat oven to 200°C (400°F/Gas 6). Line a baking tray with baking paper.

**2** Put the chickpea chips, almonds and pepitas into a bowl. Combine the tamari and sweet chilli sauce, add to the bowl and mix well to combine.

**3** Spread the mixture over the prepared tray and bake for 10–15 minutes or until the nuts and chips are crisp. Set aside to cool completely. Store in an airtight container for up to 2 weeks.

**per serve**  fat 13.7 g ▮ saturated fat 1.1 g ▮ protein 5.6 g ▮ carbohydrate 8.7 g ▮ fibre 2.8 g ▮ cholesterol 0 mg ▮ sodium 113 mg ▮ energy 773 kJ (185 Cal) ▮ gi low ▼

▮ Enjoy this high-energy snack in moderation.

sweet chilli tofu nori wraps

## carrot & walnut muffins  makes 12

| | |
|---|---|
| 1 cup (110 g/3½ oz) chickpea flour (besan) | 3 cups (465 g/15 oz) firmly packet grated carrot |
| 2½ cups (300 g/10 oz) gluten-free plain flour pre-mix | 1 cup (125 g/4 oz) chopped baking walnuts |
| 2 teaspoons gluten-free baking powder | 4 eggs, lightly beaten |
| 2 teaspoons bicarbonate of soda (baking soda) | 1 cup (250 ml/8 fl oz) light olive oil |
| 1 teaspoon mixed spice | 1 cup (260 g/8⅓ oz) gluten-free Greek-style plain yoghurt |
| 2 cups (460 g/15 oz) firmly packed brown sugar | |

**1**  Preheat oven to 190°C (375°F/Gas 5). Lightly grease two 6 x 1 cup (250 ml/8 fl oz) capacity non-stick muffin pans.
**2**  Put the flours, baking powder, bicarbonate of soda, mixed spice, brown sugar, carrot and walnuts into a large bowl and mix to combine.
**3**  Combine the eggs, olive oil and yoghurt. Gently fold into the dry ingredients until well combined.
**4**  Divide the mixture among the muffin holes. Bake for 45 minutes or until a skewer comes out clean when inserted into the centre. Turn out on a wire rack to cool.

**per muffin**  fat 30.1 g ▮ saturated fat 4.7 g ▮ protein 7.5 g ▮ carbohydrate 62.1 g ▮ fibre 3.3 g ▮ cholesterol 69 mg ▮ sodium 333 mg ▮ energy 2290 kJ (547 Cal) ▮ gi low–med ▼–◆

▮ Enjoy these muffins in moderation. The oil and brown sugar give them a high fat and calorie content. The walnuts also provide fat content, but some of it is heart-healthy omega-3 fat.

## sweet chilli tofu nori wraps  serves 4

| | |
|---|---|
| 375 g (12 oz) firm tofu | olive oil spray |
| 1 tablespoon gluten-free tamari | 8 sheets nori seaweed |
| 1 tablespoon gluten-free sweet chilli sauce | 25 g (1 oz) baby English spinach |

**1**  Cut the tofu into 1 cm (½ in) thick slices, then cut each slice into 2.5 cm (1 in) wide pieces. Put the tofu into a bowl. Combine the tamari and sweet chilli sauce, pour over the tofu and gently turn to coat. Cover and marinate for 30 minutes.
**2**  Lightly spray a non-stick fry pan with olive oil spray. Cook the tofu over medium heat for 2 minutes each side or until heated through.
**3**  Lay the nori on a work surface, top with the tofu and spinach and roll up. Cut in half to serve.

**per serve**  fat 7.1 g ▮ saturated fat 1.1 g ▮ protein 12.6 g ▮ carbohydrate 3.6 g ▮ fibre 4.4 g ▮ cholesterol 0 mg ▮ sodium 405 mg ▮ energy 573 kJ (137 Cal) ▮ gi low ▼

carrot & walnut muffins

sesame & tamari crackers

**pumpkin, ricotta & cream cheese dip**

## sesame & tamari crackers makes 28

100 g ($3^{1}/_{3}$ oz) gluten-
  free plain flour pre-mix
70 g ($2^{1}/_{4}$ oz) soy flour
2 tablespoons toasted
  sesame seeds

50 ml ($1^{2}/_{3}$ fl oz) olive oil
50 ml ($1^{2}/_{3}$ fl oz) boiling
  water
1 tablespoon gluten-free
  tamari

**1** Preheat oven to 200°C (400°F/Gas 6). Line
2 baking trays with baking paper.
**2** Put the flours and sesame seeds into a bowl and
mix to combine.
**3** Whisk together the oil, water and tamari. Slowly
pour into the dry ingredients and stir until the mixture
comes together, adding a little more water if needed.
**4** Knead the dough for 3 minutes to form a smooth
ball, cover with a dry cloth and set aside at room
temperature for 30 minutes.
**5** Roll out the dough between 2 sheets of baking
paper until 5 mm ($1/4$ in) thick. Using a 4 cm ($1^{1}/_{2}$ in)
fluted or plain cutter, cut the dough into rounds.
Place the rounds on the prepared trays and bake for
10–15 minutes or until the crackers are crisp and
golden. Transfer to a wire rack to cool.

**per cracker** fat 2.2 g ▮ saturated fat 0.3 g ▮ protein 1.4 g
▮ carbohydrate 2.9 g ▮ fibre 0.5 g ▮ cholesterol 0 mg ▮ sodium
37 mg ▮ energy 160 kJ (38 Cal) ▮ gi low–med ▼–◆

## pumpkin, ricotta & cream cheese dip serves 8–10

200 g ($6^{1}/2$ oz) peeled
  pumpkin, cut into large
  pieces
200 g ($6^{1}/2$ oz) low-fat
  ricotta cheese
30 g (1 oz) reduced-fat
  cream cheese

2 tablespoons chopped
  fresh coriander
  (cilantro)
2 tablespoons gluten-
  free sweet chilli sauce

**1** Preheat oven to 200°C (400°F/Gas 6).
**2** Place the pumpkin pieces on a non-stick baking
tray and bake for 40 minutes or until soft. Set aside
to cool.
**3** Put the cooled pumpkin, ricotta, cream cheese,
coriander and sweet chilli sauce into a food
processor and process until smooth. Serve with
gluten-free rice crackers.

**per serve (10)** fat 2.4 g ▮ saturated fat 1.5 g ▮ protein 2.8 g
▮ carbohydrate 3.5 g ▮ fibre 0.3 g ▮ cholesterol 10 mg ▮ sodium
84 mg ▮ energy 196 kJ (47 Cal) ▮ gi low ▼

**buckwheat crispbread with tuna salsa**

## pizza melts serves 4

4 rice cakes

2 tablespoons tomato
  paste

1 medium tomato, sliced

100 g (3¹/₃ oz) gluten-
  free 97% fat-free
  ham

100 g (3¹/₃ oz) canned
  pineapple pieces in
  natural juice, drained

¹/₃ cup (40 g/1¹/₃ oz)
  grated mozzarella
  cheese

2 teaspoons chopped
  fresh parsley

**1** Spread the rice cakes with the tomato paste. Top
the rice cakes with the tomato slices, ham, pineapple
and mozzarella.

**2** Cook the pizzas under a grill preheated to high
until the cheese is golden brown, watching to make
sure the rice cakes don't burn. Sprinkle with parsley
and serve immediately.

**per serve**  fat 3.5 g ▌ saturated fat 1.8 g ▌ protein 9 g
▌ carbohydrate 11.4 g ▌ fibre 1.7 g ▌ cholesterol 19 mg ▌ sodium
505 mg ▌ energy 492 kJ (118 Cal) ▌ gi med ◆

▌ You can use low-fat mozzarella cheese to reduce
the fat content of the pizzas.

## buckwheat crispbread with tuna salsa serves 4

185 g (6 oz) can tuna in
  spring water, drained

1 medium tomato, diced

1 anchovy canned in
  brine, drained and
  chopped (optional)

1 tablespoon shredded
  fresh basil

2 teaspoons balsamic
  vinegar

1 teaspoon extra virgin
  olive oil

4 buckwheat crispbread

**1** Put the tuna, tomato, anchovy, basil, vinegar and
olive oil into a bowl. Gently mix to combine.

**2** Serve the crispbread topped with the salsa.

**per serve**  fat 2.3 g ▌ saturated fat 0.6 g ▌ protein 10.4 g
▌ carbohydrate 4.6 g ▌ fibre 0.6 g ▌ cholesterol 21 mg ▌ sodium
53 mg ▌ energy 347 kJ (83 Cal) ▌ gi med–high ◆-▲

# dinner

phad thai

# phad thai serves 4–6

200 g (6½ oz) rice stick
   noodles
2 teaspoons olive oil
300 g (10 oz) firm tofu,
   cut into thin sticks
2 spring onions
   (scallions), sliced
1 medium carrot, sliced
2 medium zucchini
   (courgette), sliced
2 tablespoons water
2 tablespoons snipped
   fresh garlic chives
2 eggs, lightly beaten
¼ cup (60 ml/2 fl oz)
   fish sauce

⅓ cup (80 ml/2⅔ fl oz)
   gluten-free sweet chilli
   sauce
¼ cup (60 ml/2 fl oz)
   gluten-free tomato
   sauce
2 tablespoons lime juice
1 cup (90 g/3 oz) bean
   sprouts
2 tablespoons chopped
   fresh coriander
   (cilantro)
2 tablespoons chopped
   dry-roasted peanuts

**1**  Cover the rice noodles with boiling water and set aside for 10 minutes or until soft. Drain well.
**2**  Heat the oil in a wok over high heat. Add the tofu and cook until golden. Add the vegetables and water and stir fry for 3 minutes. Push the mixture to one side.
**3**  Add the chives and eggs and stir until scrambled.
**4**  Add the noodles, sauces and lime juice to the wok and stir fry until heated through. Remove from the heat and toss through the bean sprouts, coriander and peanuts.

per serve (6)  fat 9.1 g ▮ saturated fat 1.5 g ▮ protein 13.2 g ▮ carbohydrate 33 g ▮ fibre 3.5 g ▮ cholesterol 62 mg ▮ sodium 1229 mg ▮ energy 1151 kJ (275 Cal) ▮ gi low ▼

# honey fish with crunchy snowpeas serves 4

2 tablespoons potato
   flour
¼ teaspoon sea salt
¼ teaspoon ground
   white pepper
500 g (1 lb) firm white
   fish fillets (ling, perch),
   cut into chunks
⅓ cup (80 ml/2⅔ fl oz)
   sesame oil

2 cm (¾ in) piece fresh
   ginger, finely chopped
2 cloves garlic, crushed
200 g (6½ oz) trimmed
   snowpeas
3 tablespoons honey
2 tablespoons gluten-
   free tamari
1 tablespoon toasted
   sesame seeds

**1**  Combine the potato flour, sea salt and white pepper in a large bowl. Gently toss the fish pieces through the flour.
**2**  Heat ¼ cup (60 ml/2 fl oz) of the sesame oil in a large fry pan over medium-high heat. Cook the fish in batches for 2–3 minutes or until browned all over. Drain on absorbent paper. Set aside and keep warm.
**3**  Wipe out the fry pan and heat the remaining oil over medium heat. Sauté the ginger and garlic for 1 minute.
**4**  Add the snowpeas and stir fry for 2–3 minutes or until just tender but still crunchy. Add the honey and tamari and gently toss to coat.
**5**  Return the fish to the pan and gently toss until heated through. Toss through the sesame seeds. Serve with steamed rice.

per serve  fat 10.3 g ▮ saturated fat 1.4 g ▮ protein 26.5 g ▮ carbohydrate 26.6 g ▮ fibre 2.2 g ▮ cholesterol 41 mg ▮ sodium 792 mg ▮ energy 1281 kJ (306 Cal) ▮ gi low–med ▼–◆

honey fish with crunchy snowpeas

lamb souvlaki wraps

**rice noodles with beef & greens**

## lamb souvlaki wraps serves 4

300 g (10 oz) lean lamb
 leg steaks, cut into
 thin strips
400 g (13 oz) can
 cannellini beans,
 rinsed and drained
2 cloves garlic, crushed
2 teaspoons extra virgin
 olive oil
2 teaspoons dried
 oregano
1/4 cup (60 ml/2 fl oz)
 lemon juice
sea salt and pepper

1/4 cup (55 g/1²/3 oz)
 millet
1 medium tomato,
 chopped
1 spring onion (scallion),
 chopped
1/2 cup (10 g/1/3 oz)
 chopped fresh flat-leaf
 parsley
75 g (2¹/2 oz) mixed
 salad leaves
3 tablespoons gluten-
 free low-fat tzatziki dip
4 gluten-free white
 corn tortillas

**1** Put the lamb, cannellini beans, garlic, olive oil, oregano and 2 tablespoons of the lemon juice into a bowl. Season with sea salt and pepper and mix to combine. Cover and refrigerate overnight.
**2** Put the millet into a pan, cover with cold water and boil over medium heat for 30 minutes or until soft. Rinse under cold water and drain well.
**3** Put the drained millet, tomato, spring onion, parsley and remaining lemon juice into a bowl and mix to combine.
**4** Heat a lightly oiled barbecue grill to high. Add the lamb mixture and cook until tender.
**5** Serve the lamb mixture, millet mixture, salad leaves and tzatziki dip rolled up in the tortillas.

**per serve** fat 8.9 g ▌ saturated fat 2.9 g ▌ protein 26.4 g
▌ carbohydrate 32 g ▌ fibre 8.7 g ▌ cholesterol 52 mg ▌ sodium
156 mg ▌ energy 1382 kJ (330 Cal) ▌ gi low ▽

## rice noodles with beef & greens serves 4

2 teaspoons olive oil
500 g (1 lb) lean beef
 rump steak, thinly
 sliced
1 medium onion, sliced
200 g (6¹/2 oz) asparagus,
 cut into short lengths
1 bunch (200 g/6¹/2 oz)
 broccolini, sliced
1 bunch (200 g/6¹/2 oz)
 Chinese broccoli,
 roughly chopped

300 g (10 oz) fresh rice
 noodles, cut into
 thick strips
1/3 cup (80 ml/2²/3 fl oz)
 fish sauce
2 tablespoons gluten-
 free oyster sauce
1/4 cup (60 g/2 oz)
 grated palm sugar or
 brown sugar
1/2 teaspoon cracked
 black pepper

**1** Heat the oil in a wok over high heat. Add the beef and stir fry until browned.
**2** Add the onion and stir fry for 3 minutes or until golden. Add the asparagus, broccolini and Chinese broccoli and cook for 3 minutes or until bright green.
**3** Separate the noodles, add to the wok and stir fry for 5 minutes or until the noodles are soft.
**4** Whisk together the fish sauce, oyster sauce, sugar and pepper. Stir through the noodles and cook until the sauce is heated through.

**per serve** fat 9.1 g ▌ saturated fat 2.8 g ▌ protein 37.9 g
▌ carbohydrate 52.1 g ▌ fibre 7.1 g ▌ cholesterol 80 mg ▌ sodium
2458 mg ▌ energy 1915 kJ (457 Cal) ▌ gi low ▽

dinner

chicken tortillas

## roast chicken with quinoa mushroom stuffing serves 6

4 dried shiitake
   mushrooms
1/4 cup (60 ml/2 fl oz)
   boiling water
1 1/2 cups (375 ml/
   12 fl oz) gluten-free
   chicken stock
1/3 cup (60 g/2 oz)
   quinoa
2 slices gluten-free
   white bread

1 medium onion, grated
2 slices bacon, trimmed
   and chopped
1 tablespoon chopped
   fresh lemon thyme
1 teaspoon grated lemon
   zest
1.5 kg (3 lb) organic
   chicken
1 teaspoon olive oil
sea salt and pepper

**1** Preheat oven to 200°C (400°F/Gas 6).

**2** Put the shiitake mushrooms and boiling water into a bowl and set aside for 10 minutes or until the mushrooms are soft. Remove the mushrooms from the soaking liquid and finely shred them, reserving the liquid.

**3** Put the stock and quinoa into a pan and boil over medium heat for 15 minutes or until the quinoa is soft. Transfer to a bowl.

**4** Put the bread into a food processor and process until it forms breadcrumbs. Add the breadcrumbs, mushrooms, reserved soaking liquid, onion, bacon, lemon thyme and lemon zest to the quinoa and mix to combine.

**5** Rinse the chicken and pat the skin and cavity dry with absorbent paper. Fill the cavity with the quinoa mixture. Rub the skin with the oil and generously season with sea salt and pepper.

**6** Put the chicken onto a rack in a baking dish and bake for 1 1/4 hours or until the chicken juices run clear. Set aside for 15 minutes before carving. Serve with roasted vegetables and gluten-free gravy (page 117).

per serve   fat 19.8 g ▌ saturated fat 6.1 g ▌ protein 33.8 g ▌ carbohydrate 14.6 g ▌ fibre 1.2 g ▌ cholesterol 150 mg ▌ sodium 559 mg ▌ energy 1561 kJ (373 Cal) ▌ gi low ▼

▌ To lower the fat content of this meal, serve the chicken without the skin. Any leftover stuffing can be frozen or baked in a muffin pan. The stuffing is also delicious with roast turkey.

## chicken tortillas serves 4–6

2 skinless chicken
   breast fillets
8 gluten-free white
   corn tortillas
olive oil spray
600 g (1 lb 3 oz) bottled
   tomato salsa
400 g (13 oz) can
   chopped tomatoes

1 medium green
   capsicum (bell pepper),
   chopped
1 tablespoon chopped
   bottled jalapeños
1/3 cup (85 g/2 3/4 oz)
   light sour cream
1/4 cup (30 g/1 oz)
   grated cheddar cheese

**1** Preheat oven to 200°C (400°F/Gas 6).

**2** Put the chicken in a deep fry pan, cover with water and cook over medium heat for 20 minutes or until tender. Drain, set aside to cool, then finely shred.

**3** Cut the tortillas into bite-sized pieces and arrange on a baking tray. Spray with olive oil spray and bake for 15 minutes or until crisp and golden.

**4** Put the tomato salsa, tomatoes, capsicum and jalapeños into a pan, add the tortilla chips and heat for 3 minutes or until the chips are just soft.

**5** Pour the tortilla mixture into an ovenproof dish, top with the chicken, sour cream and cheese and bake for 20 minutes. Serve with a mixed salad.

per serve (6)   fat 8.7 g ▌ saturated fat 3.7 g ▌ protein 21.2 g ▌ carbohydrate 26.5 g ▌ fibre 4.7 g ▌ cholesterol 59 mg ▌ sodium 657 mg ▌ energy 1176 kJ (281 Cal) ▌ gi low–med ▼–◆

roast chicken with quinoa mushroom stuffing

rice noodle lasagne

## rice noodle lasagne serves 6

2 teaspoons olive oil

1 medium onion, finely chopped

2 cloves garlic, crushed

500 g (1 lb) lean premium beef mince

1 medium red capsicum (bell pepper), chopped

1 medium carrot, sliced

1 medium zucchini (courgette), sliced

3 large field mushrooms, sliced

700 g (1 lb 7 oz) gluten-free chunky tomato pasta sauce

2 tablespoons tomato paste

600 g (1 lb 3 oz) fresh rice noodle sheets

150 g (5 oz) baby English spinach

1/4 cup (30 g/1 oz) grated cheddar cheese

300 g (10 oz) low-fat ricotta cheese

1/2 cup (125 ml/4 fl oz) milk

salt and pepper

**1** Preheat oven to 200°C (400°F/Gas 6).

**2** Heat the oil in a large non-stick fry pan over medium heat. Add the onion and cook for 5 minutes or until soft. Add the garlic and beef and cook for 5 minutes or until the beef is browned.

**3** Add the capsicum, carrot, zucchini and mushrooms and cook for 3 minutes or until the vegetables soften. Stir in the pasta sauce and tomato paste and simmer for 20 minutes or until thickened.

**4** Spoon a little of the sauce over the base of a 28 cm x 21 cm (11 in x 8 1/2 in) ovenproof dish. Top with a layer of rice noodle sheets. Spoon half the beef mixture over the noodle sheets and cover with another layer of noodle sheets, half the spinach and half the grated cheese. Top with another layer of noodle sheets and the remaining beef. Add a final layer of noodle sheets and the remaining spinach.

**5** Whisk together the ricotta and milk and season with salt and pepper. Spoon over the spinach and sprinkle with the remaining grated cheese. Bake the lasagne for 45 minutes or until heated through and golden. Set aside for 15 minutes before serving with a green salad.

**per serve**  fat 16.2 g ▌ saturated fat 7.8 g ▌ protein 30.1 g ▌ carbohydrate 33.8 g ▌ fibre 5.2 g ▌ cholesterol 74 mg ▌ sodium 625 mg ▌ energy 1731 kJ (413 Cal) ▌ gi low–med ▼–◆

**pasta with rocket pesto & prosciutto**

## pasta with rocket pesto & prosciutto serves 4

1/2 cup (90 g/3 oz) toasted pine nuts

2 cups (40 g/1 1/3 oz) fresh basil leaves

60 g (2 oz) rocket (arugula), roughly torn

4 cloves garlic, roughly chopped

2 tablespoons grated parmesan cheese

salt and pepper

1/4 cup (60 ml/2 fl oz) extra virgin olive oil

50 g (1 2/3 oz) prosciutto

500 g (1 lb) gluten-free rice and corn macaroni

150 g (5 oz) baby rocket (arugula)

150 g (5 oz) low-fat semi-dried tomatoes

**1** Process the pine nuts, basil, torn rocket, garlic, parmesan, salt and pepper in a food processor until well combined. With the motor running, gradually add the oil and process until thick and creamy.

**2** Cook the prosciutto under a grill preheated to high until crisp. Break into pieces.

**3** Cook the macaroni in a large pan of rapidly boiling water until just tender. Rinse under hot water; drain.

**4** Return the drained pasta to the pan and add the pesto, baby rocket, semi-dried tomatoes and crispy prosciutto. Gently toss to combine.

**per serve**  fat 34 g ▌ saturated fat 4.1 g ▌ protein 20.4 g ▌ carbohydrate 106.7 g ▌ fibre 9 g ▌ cholesterol 10 mg ▌ sodium 316 mg ▌ energy 3336 kJ (797 Cal) ▌ gi med–high ◆–▲

nasi goreng

## sesame & roasted pumpkin tart  serves 6–8

50 g (1²/₃ oz) gluten-free
  plain flour pre-mix
100 g (3¹/₃ oz) amaranth
  flour
2 tablespoons toasted
  sesame seeds
50 ml (1²/₃ fl oz) olive oil
75 ml (2¹/₂ fl oz) boiling
  water
1 tablespoon gluten-free
  reduced-salt tamari

800 g (1 lb 10 oz) peeled
  Jap pumpkin, cut into
  large pieces
1 tablespoon gluten-free
  sweet chilli sauce
300 g (10 oz) baby
  English spinach
300 g (10 oz) silken tofu,
  drained
2 teaspoons white miso
  paste
cracked black pepper

**1**  Preheat oven to 200°C (400°F/Gas 6).

**2**  Put the flours and sesame seeds into a bowl and
mix to combine. Whisk together the oil, boiling water
and tamari. Slowly pour into the dry ingredients and
stir until the mixture comes together.

**3**  Knead the pastry for 3 minutes to form a smooth
ball, cover with a dry cloth and set aside at room
temperature for 30 minutes.

**4**  Meanwhile, put the pumpkin on a non-stick baking
tray and bake for 30 minutes or until soft. Remove
from the oven and drizzle with the sweet chilli sauce.

**5**  Roll out the pastry between 2 sheets of baking
paper until 1 cm (¹/₂ in) thick and cut to fit a deep
20 cm (8 in) loose-based tart tin. Prick the pastry
base with a fork and bake for 20 minutes or until
crisp and golden.

**6**  Steam the spinach until wilted. Cool, then
squeeze out any moisture. Spoon the spinach into
the pastry shell and top with the pumpkin.

**7**  Put the tofu and miso paste into a food processor
and process until combined. Pour over the pumpkin
and bake for 15–20 minutes or until set. Sprinkle the
top with cracked black pepper.

**per serve (8)**  fat 8.8 g ▮ saturated fat 1.5 g ▮ protein 8.4 g
▮ carbohydrate 20.1 g ▮ fibre 3.4 g ▮ cholesterol 0 mg ▮ sodium
190 mg ▮ energy 833 kJ (199 Cal) ▮ gi med ◆

▮ Cut out any leftover pastry using round or shaped
cutters and bake on a lined baking tray until golden.

## nasi goreng  serves 4

1 tablespoon peanut oil
1 teaspoon sambal oelek
2 cloves garlic, crushed
250 g (8 oz) skinless
  chicken thigh fillets,
  finely chopped
250 g (8 oz) peeled and
  deveined green
  prawns, finely chopped
4 spring onions
  (scallions), sliced

4 cups (760 g/1¹/₂ lb)
  cold cooked white rice
2 tablespoons gluten-
  free tamari
2 teaspoons brown
  sugar
4 eggs
2 medium tomatoes,
  sliced
1 medium Lebanese
  cucumber, unpeeled,
  sliced

**1**  Heat the oil in a wok over high heat, add the
sambal oelek, garlic, chicken and prawns and stir fry
until the chicken is golden.

**2**  Add the spring onions and rice and stir fry for
5 minutes or until the rice is heated through.

**3**  Stir in the combined tamari and brown sugar and
cook until heated through. Divide the rice mixture
among 4 bowls.

**4**  Fry the eggs in batches until the whites are firm
but the centres are soft. Serve the rice topped with
an egg and slices of tomato and cucumber.

**per serve**  fat 17.6 g ▮ saturated fat 4.8 g ▮ protein 37.1 g
▮ carbohydrate 58.7 g ▮ fibre 3.1 g ▮ cholesterol 334 mg ▮ sodium
1000 mg ▮ energy 2299 kJ (549 Cal) ▮ gi med–high ◆–▲

▮ You will need 1¹/₃ cups (265 g/8¹/₂ oz) uncooked
rice for this recipe.

sesame & roasted pumpkin tart

dessert

## apple pie serves 8

1 cup (120 g/4 oz)
amaranth flour
1 cup (125 g/4 oz)
gluten-free cornflour
½ cup (25 g/1 oz) baby
rice cereal
¼ cup (35 g/1 oz) pure
icing sugar
125 g (4 oz) cold butter,
chopped
2 egg whites

1–2 tablespoons iced
water
800 g (1 lb 10 oz) can
gluten-free pie apple
1 teaspoon ground
cinnamon
½ cup (125 g/4 oz)
caster sugar, plus
extra, for sprinkling
1 teaspoon reduced-fat
milk

**1** Put the flours, rice cereal and icing sugar into a bowl and mix to combine. Using your fingertips, rub the butter into the flour mixture until the mixture resembles fine breadcrumbs. Make a well in the centre and stir in the egg whites and water with a flat-bladed knife until the pastry comes together.
**2** Divide the pastry into 2 portions, one a little larger than the other. Roll out the larger portion between 2 sheets of baking paper to line a 23 cm (9 in) ovenproof glass or ceramic pie dish. Trim off any excess pastry with a sharp knife and reserve the trimmings. Roll out the remaining pastry between 2 sheets of baking paper to fit the top of the dish. Refrigerate the pastry for 20 minutes.
**3** Preheat oven to 210°C (415°F/Gas 6–7).
**4** Put the apple, cinnamon and sugar into a bowl and mix to combine.
**5** Spoon the apple mixture into the pastry shell and brush the pastry rim with the milk. Arrange the pastry lid over the apple and seal the edges with a fork. Decorate with shapes cut from the pastry trimmings. Cut a steam hole in the top, brush with milk and sprinkle with the extra sugar.
**6** Bake the pie for 10 minutes. Reduce the oven to 180°C (350°F/Gas 4) and bake for 30 minutes or until golden brown. Serve warm with gluten-free ice cream.

**per serve** fat 13.8 g ▮ saturated fat 8.5 g ▮ protein 3.5 g ▮ carbohydrate 56.2 g ▮ fibre 2.8 g ▮ cholesterol 40 mg ▮ sodium 129 mg ▮ energy 1517 kJ (362 Cal) ▮ gi med ◆

## lychee & kiwifruit granita serves 4–6

565 g (1 lb 2 oz) can
lychees in light syrup
4 kiwifruit, peeled and
chopped
½ cup (125 g/4 oz)
caster sugar

300 ml (10 fl oz)
unsweetened apple
juice
¼ cup (60 ml/2 fl oz)
lime juice

**1** Put the undrained lychees and kiwifruit into a blender and blend until smooth. Transfer to a bowl, add the sugar, apple juice and lime juice and mix to combine.
**2** Pour the mixture into a shallow metal container, cover and freeze for 2 hours or until the edges are just frozen.
**3** Scrape the mixture with a fork to break up the ice crystals, then return to the freezer for 1 hour. Repeat the scraping and freezing 5 times over the next 5 hours or until the ice crystals are even. Scrape the granita with a fork to break it up. Serve in glasses.

**per serve (6)** fat 0.2 g ▮ saturated fat 0 g ▮ protein 1.4 g ▮ carbohydrate 47.5 g ▮ fibre 3 g ▮ cholesterol 0 mg ▮ sodium 14 mg ▮ energy 834 kJ (199 Cal) ▮ gi med ◆

**pavlova**

## coconut & mango bread pudding serves 6–8

4 thick slices gluten-free
  white bread
2 mangoes, thinly sliced
90 g (3 oz) gluten-free
  coconut macaroons
2 eggs, lightly beaten
¾ cup (185 ml/6 fl oz)
  milk

2 tablespoons caster
  sugar
1 teaspoon vanilla
  extract
pure icing sugar, for
  dusting

**1** Preheat oven to 180°C (350°F/Gas 4). Line the base and side of a 20 cm (8 in) spring form tin with baking paper. Put the tin onto a baking tray.
**2** Cover the base of the prepared tin with the bread, cutting the slices to fit. Arrange the mangoes and macaroons in a spiral pattern over the bread, making sure they fit tightly.
**3** Whisk together the eggs, milk, sugar and vanilla. Pour over the mangoes and macaroons and set aside for 15 minutes.
**4** Bake the pudding for 35–40 minutes or until the custard is set. Cool slightly before dusting with icing sugar and cutting into wedges.

**per serve (8)** fat 5.2 g ▮ saturated fat 3.1 g ▮ protein 5.2 g ▮ carbohydrate 32.9 g ▮ fibre 1.8 g ▮ cholesterol 53 mg ▮ sodium 250 mg ▮ energy 849 kJ (203 Cal) ▮ gi med ◆

▮ Use reduced- or low-fat milk if preferred.

## pavlova serves 8

6 egg whites, at room
  temperature
1½ cups (375 g/12 oz)
  caster sugar
½ cup (125 ml/4 fl oz)
  cream, whipped

½ cup (125 ml/4 fl oz)
  gluten-free vanilla
  custard
3 medium bananas,
  sliced
4 passionfruit

**1** Preheat oven to 160°C (315°F/Gas 2–3). Line a large baking tray with baking paper.
**2** Whisk the egg whites in a clean, dry bowl until soft peaks form. Gradually add the sugar and beat until stiff and glossy.
**3** Spread the meringue onto the prepared tray and shape into a circle. Smooth the top and side using a spatula. Bake for 5 minutes, then reduce the oven to 120°C (250°F/Gas ½) and bake for 1 ¼ hours. Carefully slide the paper and pavlova onto a wire rack to cool completely before serving.
**4** Spoon the combined cream and custard over the pavlova and top with the bananas and passionfruit.

**per serve** fat 7.3 g ▮ saturated fat 4.8 g ▮ protein 4.4 g ▮ carbohydrate 57.9 g ▮ fibre 2.1 g ▮ cholesterol 23 mg ▮ sodium 61 mg ▮ energy 1296 kJ (310 Cal) ▮ gi low–med ▼–◆

**kaffir lime & lemon grass rice pudding**

## caramel maple cheesecake serves 8–10

180 g (6 oz) gluten-free
  cookies, roughly
  crushed
1/2 cup (55 g/1 2/3 oz)
  almond meal
60 g (2 oz) butter or
  margarine, melted
250 g (8 oz) cream
  cheese, softened
1/2 cup (115 g/3 2/3 oz)
  firmly packed brown
  sugar

250 g (8 oz) ricotta
  cheese
2 tablespoons pure
  maple syrup
3 eggs
1 tablespoon gluten-free
  cornflour
30 g (1 oz) butter, extra
1/4 cup (60 g/2 oz) firmly
  packed brown sugar,
  extra
1/3 cup (80 ml/2 2/3 fl oz)
  light cream

**1** Preheat oven to 160°C (315°F/Gas 2–3). Grease a 20 cm (8 in) spring form tin and line the base.
**2** Put the cookies, almond meal and melted butter into a food processor and process until the mixture just comes together. Press firmly into the base of the prepared tin. Refrigerate the base while you prepare the filling.
**3** Put the cream cheese and brown sugar into a clean food processor and process until the mixture is pale and creamy. Add the ricotta and maple syrup and process until combined, scraping the side of the bowl if needed.
**4** Add the eggs one at a time, processing well after each addition. Add the cornflour and process until combined. The mixture will appear quite thin.
**5** Pour the mixture over the prepared base and bake for 45–50 minutes or until firm and set. Cool completely before removing from the tin.
**6** Meanwhile, put the extra butter, extra brown sugar and cream into a small pan and stir over low heat until the sugar has dissolved. Simmer for 2 minutes or until the mixture has thickened. Set aside to cool completely, then refrigerate until required.
**7** Spread the topping over the cold cheesecake.

**per serve (10)** fat 29.5 g ▮ saturated fat 15.4 g ▮ protein 9.7 g
▮ carbohydrate 32.7 g ▮ fibre 1.2 g ▮ cholesterol 117 mg ▮ sodium
334 mg ▮ energy 1800 kJ (430 Cal) ▮ gi low ▼

## kaffir lime & lemon grass rice pudding serves 4

4 cups (1 litre/32 fl oz)
  calcium-enriched
  reduced- or low-fat
  milk
4 kaffir lime leaves, torn
2 lemon grass stalks,
  white part only, halved
  and bruised

1/3 cup (75 g/2 1/2 oz)
  grated palm sugar or
  brown sugar
1/2 cup (110 g/3 1/2 oz)
  short-grain rice
200 g (6 1/2 oz) red
  papaya, chopped
1 teaspoon lime juice

**1** Put the milk into a pan and heat until almost boiling. Add the kaffir lime leaves, lemon grass and sugar and stir until the sugar has dissolved.
**2** Add the rice and stir for 1 minute or until the mixture returns to the boil. Reduce the heat to low and simmer, stirring occasionally, for 30–40 minutes or until the rice is tender.
**3** Discard the lime leaves and lemon grass. Divide the rice among 4 small bowls. Serve topped with the papaya and drizzled with the lime juice.

**per serve** fat 2.3 g ▮ saturated fat 1.3 g ▮ protein 13.1 g
▮ carbohydrate 59 g ▮ fibre 1.4 g ▮ cholesterol 14 mg ▮ sodium
147 mg ▮ energy 1284 kJ (307 Cal) ▮ gi med ◆

upside-down banana polenta puddings

**rosewater strawberries with yoghurt**

## upside-down banana polenta puddings serves 4

²/₃ cup (170 ml/5²/₃ fl oz)
   pure maple syrup
4 sugar bananas, sliced
   lengthwise
4 cups (1 litre/32 fl oz)
   milk
40 g (1¹/₃ oz) butter,
   melted

¹/₃ cup (75 g/2¹/₂ oz)
   firmly packed brown
   sugar
³/₄ cup (110 g/3¹/₂ oz)
   fine polenta (cornmeal)
1 egg, lightly beaten

**1** Preheat oven to 160°C (315°F/Gas 2–3). Lightly grease 4 x 1 cup (250 ml/8 fl oz) capacity ramekins.
**2** Divide the maple syrup among the ramekins and top with the sliced bananas, trimming them to fit.
**3** Heat the milk, butter and sugar in a pan over medium heat until just simmering. Whisk in the polenta and cook, stirring constantly, for 15 minutes or until the polenta is thick and creamy. Remove from the heat and stir in the egg.
**4** Spoon the mixture into the ramekins and smooth the surface. Bake for 25 minutes or until set. Invert the warm puddings onto plates and serve with gluten-free custard.

**per serve**  fat 20 g ▍ saturated fat 12.3 g ▍ protein 14.2 g
▍ carbohydrate 116.5 g ▍ fibre 5.2 g ▍ cholesterol 106 mg
▍ sodium 205 mg ▍ energy 2929 kJ (700 Cal) ▍ gi low–med ▼–◆

▍ Use reduced- or low-fat milk if preferred.

## rosewater strawberries with yoghurt serves 4

¹/₃ cup (30 g/1 oz)
   flaked almonds
2 teaspoons caster
   sugar
¹/₄ teaspoon ground
   cardamom
250 g (8 oz)
   strawberries, halved

¹/₄ cup (60 ml/2 fl oz)
   unsweetened apple
   and blackcurrant juice
1 teaspoon rosewater
1 teaspoon orange-
   flower water
400 g (13 oz) gluten-free
   Greek-style plain
   yoghurt

**1** Put the almonds, sugar and cardamom into a bowl and mix to combine.
**2** Put the strawberries into a non-metallic bowl, add the juice, rosewater and orange-flower water and gently mix to combine.
**3** Spoon the yoghurt into 4 bowls and top with the strawberries and almond mixture.

**per serve**  fat 11.2 g ▍ saturated fat 4.9 g ▍ protein 8.1 g
▍ carbohydrate 14.8 g ▍ fibre 2.1 g ▍ cholesterol 28 mg ▍ sodium
69 mg ▍ energy 827 kJ (198 Cal) ▍ gi low ▼

dessert

**toffee poached pears**

## brandy walnut cake   serves 8–10

150 g (5 oz) baking
  walnuts
4 eggs
1¹/₂ cups (345 g/11¹/₂ oz)
  firmly packed brown
  sugar
¹/₂ cup (125 ml/4 fl oz)
  walnut oil
¹/₂ cup (135 g/4¹/₂ oz)
  apple puree
¹/₄ cup (60 ml/2 fl oz)
  brandy

¹/₂ teaspoon vanilla
  essence
2¹/₂ cups (300 g/10 oz)
  gluten-free plain flour
  pre-mix
2 teaspoons gluten-free
  baking powder
2 teaspoons bicarbonate
  of soda (baking soda)
¹/₂ teaspoon ground
  cinnamon

**1** Preheat oven to 160°C (315°F/Gas 2–3). Grease a 23 cm (9 in) spring form tin and line the base. Reserve 2 tablespoons of the walnuts for the top of the cake.
**2** Put the eggs and sugar into a large mixing bowl and beat until thick and creamy. Gently fold in the walnuts, walnut oil, apple puree, brandy and vanilla.
**3** In a separate bowl, combine the flour, baking powder, bicarbonate of soda and cinnamon. Very gently fold into the egg mixture until well combined.
**4** Pour into the prepared tin and sprinkle with the reserved walnuts. Bake for 1 hour 10 minutes or until the cake is firm and a skewer comes out clean when inserted into the centre. Cool slightly before slicing. Serve with gluten-free ice cream or custard.

**per serve (10)**  fat 23.4 g ▮ saturated fat 2.3 g ▮ protein 5.1 g ▮ carbohydrate 54.9 g ▮ fibre 2 g ▮ cholesterol 75 mg ▮ sodium 275 mg ▮ energy 1916 kJ (458 Cal) ▮ gi med ◆

▮ If you can't find walnut oil, use a good-quality olive oil.

## toffee poached pears   serves 4

4 medium pears, peeled
  and cored
1 cinnamon stick
1 vanilla bean, halved
  lengthwise

2 star anise
2 cups (500 ml/16 fl oz)
  unsweetened apple
  juice
1 cup (250 g/8 oz) sugar

**1** Cut the bases off the pears so they will stand upright. Place into a pan and add the cinnamon stick, vanilla bean, star anise and apple juice. Cover and cook over medium heat for 15–20 minutes or until the pears are soft. Transfer the pears to a wire rack and strain the cooking liquid, reserving 1 cup (250 ml/8 fl oz).
**2** Put the sugar and cooking liquid into a pan and stir over low heat until the sugar has dissolved. Bring to the boil and cook until the liquid turns deep golden. Working quickly, drizzle the toffee over the pears. Allow to cool and set. Serve with gluten-free custard or ice cream.

**per serve**  fat 0.2 g ▮ saturated fat 0 g ▮ protein 0.5 g ▮ carbohydrate 96.9 g ▮ fibre 3.1 g ▮ cholesterol 0 mg ▮ sodium 15 mg ▮ energy 1598 kJ (382 Cal) ▮ gi low ▼

brandy

# breads & baking

anzac biscuits

# fruit buns

canola oil spray
450 g (15 oz) gluten-free
   bread mix
1/4 cup (40 g/1 1/3 oz)
   lightly packed brown
   sugar
1/4 cup (60 ml/2 fl oz)
   olive oil
1 egg, lightly beaten

1 2/3 cups (420 ml/
   14 fl oz) water
1 1/2 teaspoons mixed
   spice
1 cup (120 g/4 oz)
   sultanas or other
   chopped dried fruit
1 tablespoon caster
   sugar

**1** Preheat oven to 210°C (415°F/Gas 6–7). Line 16 x 1/2 cup (125 ml/4 fl oz) capacity muffin holes with muffin cases. Spray the muffin cases with canola oil spray.

**2** Put the bread mix, brown sugar, olive oil, egg, 360 ml (12 fl oz) of the water and 1 teaspoon of the mixed spice into a large bowl. Mix with an electric mixer on low-medium speed for 4–5 minutes or until smooth. Stir in the sultanas.

**3** Divide the mixture among the muffin cases. Set aside for 10 minutes, then bake for 10–12 minutes or until light golden brown.

**4** Meanwhile, put the remaining water, remaining mixed spice and caster sugar into a pan. Cook over medium heat, stirring constantly, for 2–3 minutes or until the sugar has dissolved.

**5** Brush the glaze over the hot fruit buns as soon as they are removed from the oven. Set aside for 5 minutes before transferring to a wire rack to cool. Serve warm with butter. The buns can be frozen and thawed in the microwave.

**per bun** fat 4.7 g ▌ saturated fat 0.6 g ▌ protein 2.9 g ▌ carbohydrate 31.3 g ▌ fibre 2 g ▌ cholesterol 12 mg ▌ sodium 140 mg ▌ energy 751 kJ (179 Cal) ▌ gi med ◈

▌ To lower the GI of the buns, use dried apricots, dried pear, dried peach, dried apple, dried fruit medley or prunes instead of sultanas. Using a bread mix that contains a higher proportion of soy flour and less glucose will also help lower the GI.

# anzac biscuits

2 cups (60 g/2 oz)
   gluten-free cornflakes
3/4 cup (70 g/2 1/4 oz)
   desiccated coconut
1 cup (250 g/8 oz) sugar
1 1/2 cups (180 g/6 oz)
   gluten-free plain flour
   pre-mix

125 g (4 oz) butter
1 tablespoon golden
   syrup or corn syrup
1 1/2 teaspoons
   bicarbonate of soda
   (baking soda)
2 tablespoons boiling
   water

**1** Preheat oven to 150°C (300°F/Gas 2). Line 2 baking trays with baking paper.

**2** Combine the cornflakes, coconut, sugar and flour in a bowl.

**3** Melt the butter and golden syrup in a small pan over low heat. Stir the bicarbonate of soda into the boiling water until completely dissolved. Add to the butter mixture, pour into the dry ingredients and mix to combine.

**4** Roll teaspoons of the mixture into balls and place on the prepared trays, allowing room for spreading. Flatten slightly with a fork and bake for 20 minutes or until golden brown. Cool slightly on the trays, then transfer to a wire rack to cool completely.

**per biscuit** fat 3.7 g ▌ saturated fat 2.7 g ▌ protein 0.3 g ▌ carbohydrate 11 g ▌ fibre 0.4 g ▌ cholesterol 8 mg ▌ sodium 82 mg ▌ energy 325 kJ (78 Cal) ▌ gi med ◈

fruit buns

choc-cherry loaf

**grainy bread**

## choc-cherry loaf    serves 12

¼ cup (60 ml/2 fl oz) olive oil

3 eggs

380 ml (12 fl oz) tepid water

1 teaspoon white vinegar

375 g (12 oz) rice flour

150 g (5 oz) brown rice flour

1 tablespoon xanthan gum

⅓ cup (30 g/1 oz) cocoa powder

30 g (1 oz) desiccated coconut

60 g (2 oz) brown sugar

50 g (1²/₃ oz) sugar

¼ cup (25 g/1 oz) skim or soy milk powder

1 teaspoon salt

2 teaspoons dried yeast

1 x 55 g (1²/₃ oz) Cherry Ripe® chocolate bar, roughly chopped, frozen

50 g (1²/₃ oz) chopped glacé cherries, frozen

100 g (3¹/₃ oz) choc bits, frozen

**1** Set the bread maker to Wholewheat Rapid program, 1 kg–1.25 kg loaf, dark crust; or Gluten Free program, 1.25 kg loaf, dark crust.

**2** Put the oil, eggs, water and vinegar into the bread pan. Put the remaining ingredients into a bowl, mix well and add to the pan on top of the wet ingredients.

**3** Close the lid, press Start and allow to knead for 7 minutes. Lift the lid (do not pause or turn off the machine) and use a spatula to scrape down the sides of the pan and mix the ingredients until well combined. The dough should resemble mashed potato; if necessary, slowly add extra rice flour or water until it reaches this consistency. Close the lid and continue cooking.

**4** When cooked, remove the bread from the bread machine within 10 minutes. Set aside in the pan for 5–7 minutes before turning out on a wire rack to cool. The bread can be frozen.

**per serve**  fat 12.2 g ▌ saturated fat 5.1 g ▌ protein 6.5 g ▌ carbohydrate 54.6 g ▌ fibre 2.5 g ▌ cholesterol 48 mg ▌ sodium 244 mg ▌ energy 1503 kJ (359 Cal) ▌ gi med ◆

▌ The chocolate bar, cherries and choc bits need to be frozen so they remain suspended in the mixture.

## grainy bread    serves 15

⅓ cup (80 ml/2²/₃ fl oz) oil

3 eggs

450 ml (15 fl oz) tepid water

1 teaspoon white vinegar

380 g (12 oz) rice flour

100 g (3¹/₃ oz) brown rice flour

120 g (4 oz) arrowroot

70 g (2¼ oz) chickpea flour (besan)

3 tablespoons seeds (linseeds/flaxseeds, sunflower seeds, pepitas/pumpkin seeds, sesame seeds)

1 tablespoon xanthan gum

1½ tablespoons sugar

1½ teaspoons salt

2½ teaspoons dried yeast

**1** Set the bread maker to Basic Rapid or Turbo program, 1 kg–1.25 kg loaf, dark crust; or Gluten Free program, 1.25 kg loaf, dark crust.

**2** Put the oil, eggs, water and vinegar into the bread pan. Add the dry ingredients in the given order.

**3** Close the lid, press Start and allow to knead for 7 minutes. Lift the lid (do not pause or turn off the machine) and use a spatula to scrape down the sides of the pan and mix the ingredients until well combined. The dough should resemble mashed potato; if necessary, slowly add extra rice flour or water until it reaches this consistency. Close the lid and continue cooking.

**4** When cooked, remove the bread from the bread machine within 10 minutes. Set aside in the pan for 5–7 minutes before turning out on a wire rack to cool.

**per serve**  fat 6.9 g ▌ saturated fat 1.1 g ▌ protein 4.9 g ▌ carbohydrate 35.3 g ▌ fibre 1.8 g ▌ cholesterol 37 mg ▌ sodium 260 mg ▌ energy 970 kJ (232 Cal) ▌ gi med–high ◆–▲

apple tea cake

## apple tea cake serves 10

| | |
|---|---|
| 60 g (2 oz) reduced-fat margarine | ½ cup (125 ml/4 fl oz) skim or no-fat milk |
| 1 cup (250 g/8 oz) caster sugar | 50 g (1²/₃ oz) apple puree |
| 1 egg, lightly beaten | 10 g (¹/₃ oz) reduced-fat margarine, melted, extra |
| 1 teaspoon vanilla essence | |
| ¾ cup (85 g/2³/₄ oz) gluten-free self-raising flour | 1 tablespoon caster sugar, extra |
| ½ teaspoon xanthan gum | 1 teaspoon ground cinnamon |
| 3 tablespoons baby rice cereal | |

**1** Preheat oven to 180°C (350°F/Gas 4). Grease and line a 20 cm (8 in) round cake tin.
**2** Beat the margarine and sugar together until creamy. Gradually add the egg, beating well after each addition. Beat in the vanilla.
**3** Sift together the flour and xanthan gum. Fold into the egg mixture, along with the rice cereal and milk.
**4** Spoon half the batter into the prepared tin. Spread the apple puree over the top, then top with the remaining batter. Smooth the surface and bake for 30 minutes or until a skewer comes out clean when inserted into the centre.
**5** Brush the extra margarine over the warm cake and sprinkle with the combined extra sugar and ground cinnamon.

**per serve** fat 4.8 g ▌ saturated fat 0.8 g ▌ protein 1.3 g ▌ carbohydrate 34.4 g ▌ fibre 0.6 g ▌ cholesterol 19 mg ▌ sodium 41 mg ▌ energy 764 kJ (183 Cal) ▌ gi med ◆

## pumpkin, fetta & rosemary corn bread serves 8–10

| | |
|---|---|
| 400 g (13 oz) peeled pumpkin, cut into thin wedges | 100 g (3¹/₃ oz) fetta cheese, crumbled |
| 1¼ cups (145 g/4³/₄ oz) gluten-free self-raising flour | ½ cup (50 g/1²/₃ oz) grated parmesan cheese |
| ¾ cup (110 g/3¹/₂ oz) fine polenta (cornmeal) | 1 teaspoon chopped fresh rosemary |
| 2 teaspoons gluten-free baking powder | 2 eggs, lightly beaten |
| 1 teaspoon xanthan gum | 1 cup (250 ml/8 fl oz) buttermilk |
| 1 teaspoon salt | 2 tablespoons olive oil |
| | 4 fresh rosemary sprigs |
| | sea salt and pepper |

**1** Preheat oven to 200°C (400°F/Gas 6). Line a 10 cm x 23 cm (4 in x 9 in) loaf tin with baking paper.
**2** Put the pumpkin on a non-stick baking tray and bake for 30 minutes or until tender.
**3** Put the flour, polenta, baking powder, xanthan gum, salt, fetta, parmesan and chopped rosemary into a large bowl and mix to combine. Make a well in the centre.
**4** Whisk together the eggs, buttermilk and oil, pour into the well and mix until well combined.
**5** Spoon the mixture into the prepared loaf tin, top with the pumpkin and rosemary sprigs and sprinkle with sea salt and pepper. Bake for 45 minutes or until a skewer comes out clean when inserted into the centre.

**per serve (10)** fat 9.6 g ▌ saturated fat 3.9 g ▌ protein 7.9 g ▌ carbohydrate 21.2 g ▌ fibre 1.1 g ▌ cholesterol 51 mg ▌ sodium 523 mg ▌ energy 855 kJ (204 Cal) ▌ gi med ◆

pumpkin, fetta & rosemary corn bread

shortbread creams

banana honey cake

## shortbread creams makes 18

220 g (7 oz) butter, chopped

1/2 cup (125 g/4 oz) caster sugar

1/2 cup (70 g/2 1/4 oz) pure icing sugar, sifted

2 teaspoons vanilla essence

2 eggs

1 cup (120 g/4 oz) gluten-free plain flour pre-mix

3/4 cup (120 g/4 oz) rice flour

1/2 cup (80 g/2 2/3 oz) potato flour

1 cup (50 g/1 2/3 oz) baby rice cereal

1/2 cup (65 g/2 oz) gluten-free custard powder

1 teaspoon xanthan gum

30 g (1 oz) butter, extra

200 g (6 1/2 oz) pure icing sugar, sifted, extra

1 teaspoon hot water

**1** Preheat oven to 180°C (350°F/Gas 4). Line 2 large baking trays with baking paper.

**2** Beat the butter, caster sugar, icing sugar and vanilla in a large bowl until creamy. Add the eggs and mix well.

**3** Sift the flours, rice cereal, custard powder and xanthan gum onto the butter mixture and mix to form a stiff dough. Add more rice flour if necessary until the mixture comes together into a ball.

**4** Roll out the dough between 2 sheets of baking paper until 1 cm (1/2 in) thick. Use a small fluted cutter to cut the dough into rounds. Place on the prepared trays and bake for 12–15 minutes or until golden. Cool slightly on the trays, then transfer to a wire rack to cool completely.

**5** Beat the extra butter, extra icing sugar and hot water until creamy. Use the mixture to sandwich the biscuits together.

**per shortbread cream** fat 12.7 g ▮ saturated fat 8 g ▮ protein 1.8 g ▮ carbohydrate 39.5 g ▮ fibre 0.7 g ▮ cholesterol 57 mg ▮ sodium 161 mg ▮ energy 1162 kJ (278 Cal) ▮ gi med ◆

## banana honey cake serves 12

1 cup (115 g/3 2/3 oz) gluten-free self-raising flour

1 cup (160 g/5 1/3 oz) brown rice flour

1 teaspoon xanthan gum

1 teaspoon gluten-free baking powder

1/2 teaspoon bicarbonate of soda (baking soda)

2 teaspoons ground cinnamon

1/2 cup (45 g/1 1/2 oz) desiccated coconut

1/2 cup (65 g/2 oz) chopped walnuts

4 medium ripe bananas, mashed

3/4 cup (270 g/8 2/3 oz) honey

1/4 cup (60 ml/2 fl oz) olive oil

2 teaspoons vanilla essence

**1** Preheat oven to 180°C (350°F/Gas 4). Grease and line a 26 cm (10 1/2 in) spring form tin.

**2** Put the flours, xanthan gum, baking powder, bicarbonate of soda, cinnamon, coconut and walnuts into a bowl and mix to combine.

**3** Whisk together the bananas, honey, olive oil and vanilla. Pour into the dry ingredients and mix well.

**4** Spoon the mixture into the prepared tin and bake for 35–40 minutes or until a skewer comes out clean when inserted into the centre.

**per serve** fat 11.3 g ▮ saturated fat 3.1 g ▮ protein 2.7 g ▮ carbohydrate 41.5 g ▮ fibre 2.6 g ▮ cholesterol 0 mg ▮ sodium 92 mg ▮ energy 1176 kJ (281 Cal) ▮ gi low–med ▼–◆

▮ To lower the GI of the cake, use unblended yellow box honey.

olive bread

## oven-baked bread rolls makes 15

450 ml (15 fl oz) tepid
   water
$1/3$ cup (80 ml/$2^2/3$ fl oz)
   olive oil
3 eggs
1 teaspoon white vinegar
380 g (12 oz) rice flour
120 g (4 oz) arrowroot
100 g ($3^1/3$ oz) brown
   rice flour

70 g ($2^1/4$ oz) chickpea
   flour (besan) or soy
   flour
$1^1/2$ tablespoons sugar
1 tablespoon xanthan
   gum
$2^1/2$ teaspoons dried
   yeast
$1^1/2$ teaspoons salt
2 tablespoons sesame
   seeds

**1** Preheat oven to 110°C (240°F/Gas $1/2$). Grease 15 x $1/2$ cup (125 ml/4 fl oz) capacity muffin holes.
**2** Put all the ingredients, except the sesame seeds, into a large bowl and mix with an electric mixer on low-medium speed for 5–7 minutes. The dough should resemble mashed potato; if necessary, slowly add extra rice flour or water until it reaches this consistency.
**3** Cover the machine and bowl with a tea towel; do not remove the mixer blades from the bowl. Set aside to rise for 15–20 minutes, then mix again on low-medium speed for 2–3 minutes or until stiff.
**4** Divide the dough among the muffin holes and sprinkle with the sesame seeds. Place in the oven to rise for 15–20 minutes.
**5** Increase oven to 200°C (400°F/Gas 6) and bake for 15 minutes or until a skewer comes out clean when inserted into the centre. The bread rolls can be frozen.

**per roll** fat 7.7 g ▮ saturated fat 1.3 g ▮ protein 4.7 g ▮ carbohydrate 35.2 g ▮ fibre 1.7 g ▮ cholesterol 35 mg ▮ sodium 260 mg ▮ energy 993 kJ (237 Cal) ▮ gi med–high ◆–▲

▮ You can also cook the dough in 2 small greased, lined loaf tins for 40–50 minutes. Try sprinkling the tins with sesame seeds or poppy seeds before adding the dough.

## olive bread serves 10

$1/2$ cup (70 g/$2^1/4$ oz)
   anchovy-stuffed green
   olives
$1/2$ cup (70 g/$2^1/4$ oz)
   pitted kalamata olives
3 cups (360 g/12 oz)
   gluten-free plain flour
   pre-mix
1 cup (115 g/$3^2/3$ oz)
   gluten-free bread mix

1 tablespoon xanthan
   gum
1 teaspoon salt
1 teaspoon sugar
2 teaspoons dried yeast
3 eggs, lightly beaten
2 cups (500 ml/16 fl oz)
   warm water
$1/2$ cup (125 ml/4 fl oz)
   olive oil

**1** Preheat oven to 200°C (400°F/Gas 6). Lightly grease a 10 cm x 23 cm (4 in x 9 in) loaf tin.
**2** Halve 1 tablespoon of the olives to decorate the top of the bread and roughly chop the rest.
**3** Put the flour, bread mix, xanthan gum, salt, sugar and yeast into a bowl and mix to combine.
**4** Whisk together the eggs, water and olive oil. Pour into the dry ingredients and beat well with electric beaters for 5 minutes. Stir in the chopped olives.
**5** Spoon the mixture into the prepared tin and press the reserved olives into the top. Cover with lightly oiled plastic wrap and set aside to rise in a warm place for 30 minutes.
**6** Remove the plastic and bake for 40 minutes or until the bread is risen and golden.

**per serve** fat 14.1 g ▮ saturated fat 2.3 g ▮ protein 3.4 g ▮ carbohydrate 34.4 g ▮ fibre 1.8 g ▮ cholesterol 56 mg ▮ sodium 469 mg ▮ energy 1164 kJ (278 Cal) ▮ gi med ◆

oven-baked bread rolls

# christmas

spiced nuts

## fruit mince pies

1 1/2 cups (185 g/6 oz)
  gluten-free cornflour
1/4 cup (40 g/1 1/3 oz)
  brown rice flour
1/4 cup (35 g/1 oz)
  gluten-free custard
  powder
2 tablespoons caster
  sugar

125 g (4 oz) cold butter,
  chopped
1 egg white
1–2 tablespoons iced
  water
400 g (13 oz) gluten-free
  fruit mince
pure icing sugar, for
  dusting

**1** Sift the flours and custard powder into a bowl. Stir in the sugar.

**2** Using your fingertips, rub the butter into the flour mixture until the mixture resembles fine breadcrumbs.

**3** Make a well in the centre and stir in the egg white and 1 tablespoon of iced water at a time until the pastry comes together. Gather the pastry into a ball and flatten slightly.

**4** Wrap a third of the pastry in plastic wrap and refrigerate until needed. Roll out the remaining pastry between 2 sheets of baking paper until 5 mm (1/4 in) thick. Using an 8 cm (3 in) fluted cutter, cut the pastry into rounds and fit into 2 x 12-hole patty tins. Refrigerate for 20 minutes.

**5** Preheat oven to 200°C (400°F/Gas 6).

**6** Bake the pastry shells for 10–15 minutes or until golden. Spoon 2 teaspoons of the fruit mince into each pastry shell.

**7** Roll out the reserved pastry between 2 sheets of baking paper until 5 mm (1/4 in) thick. Using a small cutter, cut out shapes and place on top of the pies. Bake for 10 minutes or until golden. Set aside to cool on a wire rack before dusting with icing sugar.

**per pie** fat 5.1 g ▌ saturated fat 3.1 g ▌ protein 0.6 g ▌ carbohydrate 18.7 g ▌ fibre 0.6 g ▌ cholesterol 14 mg ▌ sodium 69 mg ▌ energy 513 kJ (123 Cal) ▌ gi med ◆

▌ Replace the butter with reduced-fat margarine if you want to lower the fat and calorie content.

## spiced nuts

300 g (10 oz) salted
  mixed nuts
1 egg white, lightly
  beaten

1 teaspoon five-spice
  powder
1/2 teaspoon cracked
  black pepper

**1** Preheat oven to 180°C (350°F/Gas 4). Line a baking tray with baking paper.

**2** Mix together the nuts, egg white, five-spice powder and pepper.

**3** Arrange the nut mixture on the prepared tray and bake for 20 minutes or until the coating is crisp. Set aside to cool slightly, then break into pieces.

**per serve** fat 16.5 g ▌ saturated fat 2.1 g ▌ protein 6.5 g ▌ carbohydrate 2.5 g ▌ fibre 2.8 g ▌ cholesterol 0 mg ▌ sodium 184 mg ▌ energy 788 kJ (188 Cal) ▌ gi low ▼

fruit mince pies

christmas pudding

## christmas pudding serves 24

125 g (4 oz) cold butter, grated

125 g (4 oz) gluten-free self-raising flour

225 g (7 oz) gluten-free fresh breadcrumbs

1 cup (50 g/1²/₃ oz) baby rice cereal

2 cups (460 g/15 oz) firmly packed brown sugar

2 teaspoons mixed spice

½ teaspoon ground cinnamon

½ teaspoon ground nutmeg

4 cups (700 g/1 lb 7 oz) mixed dried fruit

2 cups (320 g/10²/₃ oz) raisins

3 apples, peeled, cored and grated

50 g (1²/₃ oz) blanched almonds, chopped

zest of 1 orange

zest of 1 lemon

4 eggs, lightly beaten

1 cup (250 ml/8 fl oz) brandy

**1** Put the butter, flour, breadcrumbs, rice cereal, sugar and spices into a large mixing bowl and mix well to combine. Add the dried fruit, raisins, apples, almonds and citrus zest and mix well.

**2** Whisk together the eggs and brandy, pour onto the dry ingredients and beat with a wooden spoon for 3 minutes or until combined (the mixture should drop from the spoon). Cover and refrigerate overnight.

**3** Grease 2 x 3 cup (750 ml/24 fl oz) capacity pudding basins and line the bases with baking paper.

**4** Divide the pudding mixture between the prepared basins. Put 2 sheets of foil onto a work surface and top each with a sheet of greased baking paper. Make a vertical fold down the centre and place the paper and foil over the puddings, paper-side down. Secure with string.

**5** Steam on a trivet in a pan of simmering water for 8 hours, making sure the pan does not boil dry.

**6** Remove the paper and foil and replace with a clean sheet of baking paper and foil. Refrigerate until ready to serve. Steam for another 2 hours before serving warm with gluten-free custard.

**per serve** fat 6.8 g ▮ saturated fat 3.3 g ▮ protein 3.4 g ▮ carbohydrate 60.4 g ▮ fibre 3.1 g ▮ cholesterol 45 mg ▮ sodium 162 mg ▮ energy 1402 kJ (335 Cal) ▮ gi med ◆

▮ Grate the breadcrumbs from a day-old loaf of gluten-free white bread.

## fruity bombe alaska serves 8

200 g (6½ oz) mixed berries

3 medium peaches, sliced

2 medium nectarines, sliced

3 medium plums, sliced

1 tablespoon torn fresh apple mint leaves

8 scoops gluten-free vanilla ice cream

3 egg whites, lightly beaten

1 cup (250 g/8 oz) caster sugar

**1** Preheat oven to 230°C (450°F/Gas 8).

**2** Put the fruit and mint leaves into a bowl. Gently mix to combine. Spoon into a 23 cm (9 in) ovenproof glass or ceramic dish.

**3** Arrange the ice cream scoops evenly over the top of the fruit and place in the freezer.

**4** Whisk the egg whites in a clean, dry bowl until stiff peaks form. Gradually add the sugar and beat until stiff and glossy.

**5** Quickly spread the meringue over the ice cream. Bake for 10 minutes or until the meringue is just golden. Serve immediately.

**per serve** fat 4.4 g ▮ saturated fat 2.8 g ▮ protein 4.2 g ▮ carbohydrate 48.2 g ▮ fibre 2.8 g ▮ cholesterol 10 mg ▮ sodium 48 mg ▮ energy 1041 kJ (249 Cal) ▮ gi low ▼

**shortbread**

## chocolate fudge ice cream cake serves 20

400 g (13 oz) hazelnuts
250 g (8 oz) dark
  chocolate, chopped
¼ cup (60 ml/2 fl oz)
  Kahlúa or Tia Maria
150 g (5 oz) butter,
  softened

1 cup (140 g/4½ oz)
  pure icing sugar, sifted
3 eggs
8 cups (2 litres/64 fl oz)
  gluten-free good-
  quality vanilla ice
  cream

**1** Preheat oven to 200°C (400°F/Gas 6). Line the base of a 26 cm (10½ in) spring form tin with baking paper.

**2** Place the hazelnuts onto a baking tray and roast for 10 minutes or until the skins split. Wrap in a clean tea towel and set aside for 10 minutes. Rub the nuts in the tea towel to remove the skins, then roughly chop. Sprinkle half the nuts over the base of the prepared tin.

**3** Put the chocolate in a bowl over simmering water. Do not let the base of the bowl touch the water. Stir over low heat until the chocolate has melted. Add the liqueur and set aside to cool slightly.

**4** Beat the butter and sifted icing sugar until light and creamy. Add the eggs one at a time, beating well after each addition.

**5** Using a metal spoon, stir the chocolate mixture into the butter mixture until combined. Pour half of the mixture over the nuts in the tin and freeze for 30 minutes.

**6** Slightly soften the ice cream at room temperature, then spread over the chocolate mixture. Top with the remaining chocolate mixture and freeze for 1 hour.

**7** Press the remaining hazelnuts into the chocolate mixture. Cover and freeze until ready to serve.

**8** Set the ice cream cake aside at room temperature for 5 minutes before serving, being careful not to soften it too much. Open the spring form tin and remove the outer ring from the base, running a knife around the inside to loosen it if necessary.

**per serve** fat 29.4 g ▮ saturated fat 12.5 g ▮ protein 6.5 g ▮ carbohydrate 26.9 g ▮ fibre 2.7 g ▮ cholesterol 62 mg ▮ sodium 107 mg ▮ energy 1664 kJ (397 Cal) ▮ gi low ▼

▮ Using low-fat vanilla ice cream will significantly lower the fat and calorie content of this dessert.

## shortbread makes 24

250 g (8 oz) butter,
  softened
125 g (4 oz) pure icing
  sugar

375 g (12 oz) gluten-free
  plain flour pre-mix
2 teaspoons milk
1 tablespoon sugar

**1** Preheat oven to 160°C (315°F/Gas 2–3). Line 2 baking trays with baking paper.

**2** Beat the butter and icing sugar until light and creamy. Add the flour and stir until the mixture forms a soft dough.

**3** Gently knead the dough on a lightly floured surface for 5 minutes. Roll out the dough between 2 sheets of baking paper until 1 cm (½ in) thick. Using heart or Christmas cutters, cut out shapes and place on the prepared trays.

**4** Lightly brush the top of the shortbread with the milk and sprinkle with the sugar. Bake for 15 minutes or until crisp and golden. Cool slightly on the trays, then transfer to a wire rack to cool completely.

**per shortbread** fat 8.6 g ▮ saturated fat 5.6 g ▮ protein 0.2 g ▮ carbohydrate 16 g ▮ fibre 0.3 g ▮ cholesterol 27 mg ▮ sodium 78 mg ▮ energy 587 kJ (140 Cal) ▮ gi low–med ▼–◆

chocolate fudge ice cream cake

individual christmas cakes

## individual christmas cakes makes 12

2¼ cups (395 g/13 oz) mixed dried fruit

1 cup (160 g/5⅓ oz) chopped raisins

1⅔ cups (200 g/6½ oz) sultanas

1 cup (190 g/6¼ oz) dried fruit medley

1 cup (250 ml/8 fl oz) sherry

250 g (8 oz) butter, softened

1 cup (230 g/7¼ oz) firmly packed brown sugar

4 eggs, lightly beaten

2 cups (240 g/7⅔ oz) gluten-free plain flour pre-mix

½ cup (55 g/1⅔ oz) gluten-free self-raising flour

1 cup (50 g/1⅔ oz) baby rice cereal

2 teaspoons mixed spice

1 teaspoon xanthan gum

pure icing sugar, for dusting

cake decorations

**1** Put the fruit into a large bowl and pour over the sherry. Cover with plastic wrap and soak overnight.
**2** Preheat oven to 150°C (300°F/Gas 2). Lightly grease 12 x 1 cup (250 ml/8 fl oz) capacity muffin holes and line the bases with baking paper.
**3** Beat the butter and sugar until creamy. Add the eggs one at a time, beating well after each addition. Transfer to a large bowl.
**4** Sift the flours into a bowl and stir in the rice cereal, mixed spice and xanthan gum. Stir into the butter mixture, along with the soaked fruit. Mix well.
**5** Divide the mixture among the prepared muffin holes and smooth the surface with wet fingers. Bake for 1¼ hours or until a skewer comes out clean when inserted into the centre. Turn out on a wire rack to cool completely. Lightly dust with icing sugar and top with cake decorations.

**per cake** fat 19.6 g ▌ saturated fat 12 g ▌ protein 4.8 g ▌ carbohydrate 91 g ▌ fibre 5.2 g ▌ cholesterol 116 mg ▌ sodium 226 mg ▌ energy 2407 kJ (575 Cal) ▌ gi low–med ▼–◆

▌ Some coloured cake decorations contain wheat flour, so check the ingredients carefully. The mixture can also be baked in 2 x 23 cm (9 in) round tins.

christmas punch

## christmas punch serves 10

4 cups (1 litre/32 fl oz) dry ginger ale

2 cups (500 ml/16 fl oz) unsweetened pineapple juice

2 cups (500 ml/16 fl oz) tropical fruit juice

2 tablespoons lime juice cordial

splash of Angostura bitters

500 g (1 lb) frozen mixed berries

1 tablespoon torn fresh mint leaves

**1** Put the dry ginger ale, pineapple juice, tropical fruit juice, lime juice cordial and bitters into a large jug or punch bowl and gently stir to combine. Chill until ready to serve.
**2** Add the berries and mint and stir to combine. Serve immediately.

**per serve** fat 0.2 g ▌ saturated fat 0 g ▌ protein 1.1 g ▌ carbohydrate 23.5 g ▌ fibre 1.2 g ▌ cholesterol 0 mg ▌ sodium 23 mg ▌ energy 427 kJ (102 Cal) ▌ gi low–med ▼–◆

rocky road

## spice biscuits makes 30

2 egg whites
2¼ cups (315 g/10½ oz)
    pure icing sugar,
    sifted, plus extra, for
    dusting
1½ cups (165 g/5⅓ oz)
    almond meal

1 teaspoon ground
    cinnamon
¼ teaspoon ground
    nutmeg
¼ teaspoon ground
    cloves
¼ teaspoon ground
    cardamom

**1** Preheat oven to 150°C (300°F/Gas 2). Line 2 baking trays with baking paper.
**2** Put the egg whites into a large metal bowl and beat lightly with a wooden spoon. Stir in the sifted icing sugar and mix to form a smooth paste. Remove ⅓ cup (80 ml/2⅔ fl oz) of the mixture, cover and set aside.
**3** Add the almond meal and spices to the bowl and stir until the mixture forms a smooth dough; you may need to add a little water if the dough is too dry.
**4** Roll out the dough on a surface dusted with pure icing sugar until 5 mm (¼ in) thick. Spread with the reserved icing sugar mixture and leave for 30 minutes or until the icing has set.
**5** Using a star cutter, cut the dough into star shapes. Place on the prepared trays and bake for 10 minutes or until firm and golden. Set aside to cool on the trays. Store in an airtight container for up to 2 weeks.
**per biscuit**  fat 3 g ▮ saturated fat 0.2 g ▮ protein 1.3 g ▮ carbohydrate 10.7 g ▮ fibre 0.5 g ▮ cholesterol 0 mg ▮ sodium 5 mg ▮ energy 312 kJ (75 Cal) ▮ gi med ◈

## rocky road makes 24 squares

150 g (5 oz) gluten-free
    pink and white
    marshmallows
⅓ cup (10 g/⅓ oz)
    gluten-free puffed rice
⅓ cup (50 g/1⅔ oz)
    toasted almonds,
    chopped

100 g (3⅓ oz) glacé
    cherries
⅓ cup (20 g/¾ oz)
    shredded coconut
250 g (8 oz) dark
    chocolate, chopped
50 g (1⅔ oz) butter,
    chopped

**1** Grease a 20 cm (8 in) square cake tin and line with baking paper.
**2** Put the marshmallows, puffed rice, almonds, cherries and coconut into a bowl and mix to combine.
**3** Put the chocolate and butter into a heavy-based pan and stir over low heat until melted. Pour over the dry ingredients and quickly mix to combine.
**4** Spoon into the prepared tin and refrigerate until set. Cut into small squares to serve.
**per square**  fat 6.6 g ▮ saturated fat 4.6 g ▮ protein 1.2 g ▮ carbohydrate 14.3 g ▮ fibre 0.8 g ▮ cholesterol 6 mg ▮ sodium 26 mg ▮ energy 485 kJ (116 Cal) ▮ gi low ▽

spice biscuits

# party

cheese balls

# cheese balls ~~makes 36~~

500 g (1 lb) arrowroot, plus extra, for dusting
1 teaspoon sea salt
2 cups (500 ml/16 fl oz) milk
1/3 cup (80 ml/2 2/3 fl oz) olive oil
2 eggs, lightly beaten
2 1/2 cups (250 g/8 oz) finely grated parmesan cheese

**1** Preheat oven to 180°C (350°F/Gas 4). Line 2 baking trays with baking paper.
**2** Put the arrowroot and sea salt into a bowl and mix to combine. Make a well in the centre.
**3** Heat the milk and oil in a pan over medium heat until almost boiling. Pour into the well, along with the eggs, and mix to combine. Add the parmesan and mix well. Cover and refrigerate for 15 minutes.
**4** Dust your hands with arrowroot. Roll tablespoons of the mixture into balls and arrange on the prepared trays. Bake for 30–40 minutes or until crisp and golden. Serve hot.

**per ball** fat 5.2 g ▮ saturated fat 2.2 g ▮ protein 3.5 g ▮ carbohydrate 12.4 g ▮ fibre 0.1 g ▮ cholesterol 19 mg ▮ sodium 177 mg ▮ energy 463 kJ (111 Cal) ▮ gi med ◆

▮ The unbaked cheese balls can be frozen.

# tandoori chicken rolls ~~makes 24~~

150 g (5 oz) dried rice vermicelli
1 1/4 cups (325 g/10 3/4 oz) gluten-free Greek-style plain yoghurt
3 tablespoons gluten-free tandoori paste
750 g (1 1/2 lb) skinless chicken thigh fillets, cut into bite-sized pieces
24 small rice paper rounds, 16 cm (6 1/2 in) diameter
24 fresh mint leaves
3 tablespoons gluten-free mango chutney

**1** Put the vermicelli into a bowl, cover with boiling water and allow to stand for 10 minutes or until the noodles are soft. Drain and cut into short lengths.
**2** Combine 1 cup (260 g/8 1/3 oz) of the yoghurt and the tandoori paste in a bowl. Add the chicken and mix to combine. Spread the chicken out on a foil-lined baking tray. Cook under a grill preheated to high, turning a couple of times, for 5–10 minutes or until tender.
**3** Soak a rice paper round in lukewarm water until soft and place on a clean, dry tea towel. Top with 2 teaspoons of the noodles and 2 pieces of chicken. Dip a mint leaf in the remaining yoghurt and place on top of the chicken, followed by a small spoonful of mango chutney. Roll up to enclose the filling. Cover with damp absorbent paper while you prepare the remaining rolls. Serve with extra chutney.

**per roll** fat 5.5 g ▮ saturated fat 1.9 g ▮ protein 7.2 g ▮ carbohydrate 10.7 g ▮ fibre 0.5 g ▮ cholesterol 30 mg ▮ sodium 236 mg ▮ energy 509 kJ (122 Cal) ▮ gi med ◆

tandoori chicken

polenta biscuits with capsicum & fetta

## polenta biscuits with capsicum & fetta makes 24

1 cup (120 g/4 oz) gluten-free plain flour pre-mix

1/2 cup (75 g/2 1/2 oz) fine polenta (cornmeal)

1/2 teaspoon salt

125 g (4 oz) cold butter, chopped

1/4 cup (25 g/1 oz) grated parmesan cheese

1 egg, lightly beaten

2 medium red capsicums (bell peppers), halved and seeded

olive oil spray

1 tablespoon finely chopped fresh basil

2 teaspoons extra virgin olive oil

2 teaspoons balsamic vinegar

1 tablespoon gluten-free sweet chilli sauce

50 g (1 2/3 oz) soft Danish-style fetta cheese

cracked black pepper

**1** Preheat oven to 180°C (350°F/Gas 4). Line 2 baking trays with baking paper.

**2** Place the flour, polenta and salt into a large bowl. Using your fingertips, rub the butter into the flour mixture until the mixture resembles breadcrumbs. Stir in the parmesan.

**3** Add the egg and stir until the mixture forms a dough. Cover and refrigerate for at least 30 minutes.

**4** Gently roll out the dough between 2 sheets of baking paper until 5 mm (1/4 in) thick. Using a 5 cm (2 in) fluted cutter, cut the dough into 24 rounds. Place the rounds on the prepared trays and bake for 30–35 minutes or until firm and lightly browned. Transfer to a wire rack to cool.

**5** Lightly spray the capsicums with olive oil spray. Place, skin-side up, under a grill preheated to high until the skin blisters and blackens. Transfer to a plastic bag to cool. Peel away and discard the skin from the capsicums and cut the flesh into thin strips.

**6** Put the capsicums into a bowl and add the basil, olive oil, vinegar and sweet chilli sauce.

**7** Top the biscuits with some of the capsicum mixture and a little crumbled fetta and sprinkle with cracked black pepper.

per biscuit  fat 6.1 g ▌ saturated fat 3.5 g ▌ protein 1.6 g ▌ carbohydrate 6.1 g ▌ fibre 0.3 g ▌ cholesterol 24 mg ▌ sodium 138 mg ▌ energy 357 kJ (85 Cal) ▌ gi med ◆

rice crackers with wasabi prawns

## rice crackers with wasabi prawns makes 24

2 tablespoons gluten-free good-quality soy or safflower mayonnaise

1 teaspoon wasabi paste

1/4 cup (10 g/1/3 oz) fresh coriander (cilantro) sprigs, plus extra, to serve

1 teaspoon lime juice

freshly ground black pepper

24 gluten-free rice crackers

72 cooked small school prawns, peeled and deveined

**1** Put the mayonnaise, wasabi, coriander, lime juice and a good grind of black pepper into a small food processor and process until well combined.

**2** Spoon 1/2 teaspoon of the mayonnaise onto each rice cracker. Top with 3 prawns and garnish with a coriander sprig.

per cracker  fat 0.9 g ▌ saturated fat 0.1 g ▌ protein 1.4 g ▌ carbohydrate 1.7 g ▌ fibre 0.1 g ▌ cholesterol 14 mg ▌ sodium 45 mg ▌ energy 88 kJ (21 Cal) ▌ gi high ▲

marinated chicken wings

## noodle baskets with peppered beef makes 24

100 g (3¹/₃ oz) dried rice
  vermicelli
olive oil spray
300 g (10 oz) lean beef
  rump steak
1 tablespoon cracked
  black pepper

1 tablespoon pure maple
  syrup
4 tablespoons
  horseradish cream
2 tablespoons sour
  cream
25 g (1 oz) mustard
  sprouts

**1** Preheat oven to 220°C (425°F/Gas 7).

**2** Put the vermicelli into a bowl, cover with boiling water and allow to stand for 10 minutes or until the noodles are soft. Drain well.

**3** Shape the noodles into 24 small flat discs and place into shallow patty cake holes, pressing the noodles up the side. Lightly spray with olive oil spray and bake for 10 minutes or until the noodles are crisp. Set aside to cool.

**4** Coat the beef with the cracked pepper. Cook in a lightly oiled chargrill pan until medium rare. Set aside for 5 minutes before cutting into thin slices. Transfer the beef to a bowl, add the maple syrup and gently toss to coat.

**5** Divide the beef among the noodle baskets. Top with a spoonful of the combined horseradish cream and sour cream and garnish with the mustard sprouts.

**per basket** fat 1.8 g ▮ saturated fat 0.9 g ▮ protein 3.1 g ▮ carbohydrate 4 g ▮ fibre 0.2 g ▮ cholesterol 11 mg ▮ sodium 83 mg ▮ energy 191 kJ (46 Cal) ▮ gi low ▼

▮ If you are short of time you can use mini gluten-free rice cakes instead of the noodle baskets.

## marinated chicken wings serves 8-10

2 kg (4 lb) chicken wings
1 teaspoon sesame oil
2 tablespoons gluten-
  free sweet chilli sauce
2 tablespoons gluten-
  free tamari

1 tablespoon rice
  vinegar
1 tablespoon sherry or
  Chinese rice wine
1 tablespoon brown
  sugar

**1** Cut each chicken wing into 3 pieces through the joints, discarding the tips.

**2** Combine the sesame oil, sweet chilli sauce, tamari, rice vinegar, sherry and sugar in a large non-metallic bowl. Add the chicken pieces and gently mix to coat. Cover and refrigerate overnight.

**3** Preheat oven to 200°C (400°F/Gas 6).

**4** Divide the chicken wings between 2 baking dishes and bake for 30 minutes or until tender.

**per serve (10)** fat 5.4 g ▮ saturated fat 1.7 g ▮ protein 21.8 g ▮ carbohydrate 3.3 g ▮ fibre 0 g ▮ cholesterol 79 mg ▮ sodium 320 mg ▮ energy 635 kJ (152 Cal) ▮ gi low ▼

noodle baskets with peppered beef

salt & pepper squid

coconut raspberry

## salt & pepper
## squid  serves 6–8

3 tablespoons sea salt

3 tablespoons white
peppercorns

2 teaspoons caster
sugar

2 cups (250 g/8 oz)
gluten-free cornflour

1 kg (2 lb) squid hoods,
cleaned and cut into
rings

4 egg whites, lightly
beaten

peanut oil for deep
frying

**1** Use a mortar and pestle or spice grinder to grind the sea salt, white peppercorns and sugar into a fine powder. Transfer to a bowl, add the cornflour and mix to combine.

**2** Dip the squid into the egg whites, then coat in the cornflour mixture, shaking off any excess.

**3** Heat the peanut oil in a wok over medium heat for 5 minutes or until the oil starts to move. Stand a wooden chopstick in the oil. If the oil bubbles around the chopstick, it is ready.

**4** Cook the squid in batches in the oil for 2 minutes or until crisp and golden brown. Drain on absorbent paper. Serve with lime wedges.

**per serve (8)**  fat 4 g ▌ saturated fat 0.9 g ▌ protein 17.6 g ▌ carbohydrate 15.4 g ▌ fibre 0.5 g ▌ cholesterol 187 mg ▌ sodium 2719 mg ▌ energy 714 kJ (171 Cal) ▌ gi low–med ▼–◆

## coconut raspberry
## bites  makes 24

24 gluten-free coconut
macaroons

¼ cup (60 g/2 oz)
mascarpone cheese

24 fresh raspberries

**1** Top each coconut macaroon with ½ teaspoon of the mascarpone.

**2** Press a raspberry into the top of each macaroon and serve immediately.

**per bite**  fat 3.8 g ▌ saturated fat 2.6 g ▌ protein 0.5 g ▌ carbohydrate 5.6 g ▌ fibre 0.9 g ▌ cholesterol 6 mg ▌ sodium 22 mg ▌ energy 251 kJ (60 Cal) ▌ gi low–med ▼–◆

fairy cakes

## chocolate hazelnut love cake  serves 20

250 g (8 oz) butter,
    chopped
530 g (1 lb 1 oz) dark
    chocolate, chopped
150 g (5 oz) gluten-free
    self-raising flour
1¼ cups (150 g/5 oz)
    gluten-free plain flour
    pre-mix
⅔ cup (60 g/2 oz)
    cocoa powder
½ teaspoon bicarbonate
    of soda (baking soda)
2 cups (500 g/1 lb)
    caster sugar

4 eggs
½ cup (125 ml/4 fl oz)
    buttermilk
2 tablespoons olive oil
3 tablespoons chocolate
    hazelnut spread
½ cup (125 ml/4 fl oz)
    cream
2 teaspoons glycerine
2 teaspoons light corn
    syrup
pure icing sugar, for
    dusting

**1** Preheat oven to 160°C (315°F/Gas 2–3). Lightly grease a deep 22 cm (9 in) round cake tin.
**2** Melt the butter and 250 g (8 oz) of the chocolate in a heavy-based pan over low heat. Set aside to cool slightly.
**3** Sift the flours, cocoa and bicarbonate of soda into a large bowl. Stir in the sugar. Add the chocolate mixture and stir to combine. Whisk together the eggs, buttermilk and oil. Pour into the chocolate mixture and stir to combine.
**4** Pour the mixture into the prepared tin and bake for 1¾ hours or until a skewer comes out clean when inserted into the centre. Cool in the tin for 5 minutes before turning out on a wire rack to cool completely. Spread the top of the cake with the chocolate hazelnut spread.
**5** Heat the cream and remaining chocolate in a heavy-based pan over low heat until melted and smooth. Stir in the glycerine and corn syrup. Remove from the heat, cover and set aside until the mixture has cooled and thickened. Pour over the cake and allow to set. Lightly dust the cake with icing sugar in a heart shape.

per serve  fat 25.4 g ‖ saturated fat 17.1 g ‖ protein 3.7 g
‖ carbohydrate 53.5 g ‖ fibre 1.7 g ‖ cholesterol 80 mg ‖ sodium
160 mg ‖ energy 1879 kJ (449 Cal) ‖ gi low–med ▼–◆

## fairy cakes  makes 24

125 g (4 oz) butter,
    softened
¾ cup (185 g/6 oz)
    caster sugar
1 cup (115 g/3⅔ oz)
    gluten-free self-raising
    flour
1 cup (160 g/5⅓ oz)
    brown rice flour
¾ cup (185 ml/6 fl oz)
    milk

2 eggs, lightly beaten
1 teaspoon vanilla
    essence
½ cup (125 ml/4 fl oz)
    cream
pink or blue food
    colouring
pure icing sugar, for
    dusting

**1** Preheat oven to 180°C (350°F/Gas 4). Line 24 x ⅓ cup (80 ml/2⅔ fl oz) capacity muffin holes with paper cases.
**2** Put the butter, sugar, flours, milk, eggs and vanilla into a bowl and beat until combined.
**3** Divide the mixture among the cases and bake for 10–15 minutes or until golden. Transfer to a wire rack to cool completely. Cut a circle out of the top of each cake and cut each circle in half to make wings.
**4** Beat the cream until soft peaks form, then beat in a few drops of colouring. Fill the cakes with cream, arrange the wings on top and dust with icing sugar.

per cake  fat 7.4 g ‖ saturated fat 4.7 g ‖ protein 1.4 g
‖ carbohydrate 16.1 g ‖ fibre 0.4 g ‖ cholesterol 37 mg ‖ sodium
48 mg ‖ energy 71 kJ (137 Cal) ‖ gi med ◆

chocolate hazelnut love cake

# basics

## white bread makes 1 loaf

1/3 cup (80 ml/2 2/3 fl oz)
    olive oil
3 eggs
450 ml (15 fl oz) tepid
    water
1 teaspoon white vinegar
470 g (15 oz) rice flour

200 g (6 1/2 oz) arrowroot
1 tablespoon xanthan
    gum
2 tablespoons sugar
1 1/2 teaspoons salt
2 1/2 teaspoons dried
    yeast

**1** Set the bread maker to Gluten Free program,
1.25 kg loaf, dark crust; or Basic Rapid or Turbo
program, 1–1.25 kg loaf, dark crust; or Wholewheat
Rapid program, 1.25 kg loaf, med crust.
**2** Put the oil, eggs, water and vinegar into the bread
pan. Add the dry ingredients in the given order.
**3** Close the lid, press Start and allow to knead for
7 minutes. Lift the lid (do not pause or turn off the
machine) and use a spatula to scrape down the
sides of the pan and mix the ingredients until well
combined. The dough should resemble mashed
potato; if necessary, slowly add extra rice flour or
water until it reaches this consistency. Close the lid
and continue cooking.
**4** Remove the bread from the bread machine within
10 minutes. Cool in the pan for 5–7 minutes, then
cool on a wire rack. The bread can be frozen.

## cheesy herb bread makes 8

2 1/2 cups (300 g/10 oz)
    gluten-free plain flour
    pre-mix
1 cup (120 g/4 oz)
    amaranth flour
1 tablespoon xanthan
    gum
1/2 teaspoon salt
1/4 teaspoon sugar
2 teaspoons dried yeast

1/2 cup (60 g/2 oz)
    grated reduced-fat
    cheddar cheese
2 tablespoons chopped
    fresh herbs
1 egg, lightly beaten
1 3/4 cups (440 ml/
    15 fl oz) warm water
1 tablespoon olive oil

**1** Preheat oven to 230°C (450°F/Gas 8). Lightly
grease 8 x 1/2 cup (125 ml/4 fl oz) capacity loaf tins.
**2** Sift the flours into a bowl and stir in the xanthan
gum, salt, sugar, yeast, cheese and herbs. Make a
well in the centre.
**3** Whisk together the egg, water and olive oil. Pour
into the well and stir to combine. Beat the mixture
with an electric mixer for 5 minutes.
**4** Divide the mixture among the prepared tins, cover
with lightly oiled plastic wrap and set aside to rise in
a warm place for 30 minutes.
**5** Remove the plastic and bake for 25 minutes or
until crisp and golden. Cool in the tins for 5 minutes.
Serve warm with margarine. The loaves can be frozen.

basics

## pizza base  makes 1

1 cup (115 g/3²/₃ oz)
  gluten-free bread mix
¹/₂ cup (80 g/2²/₃ oz)
  brown rice flour, plus
  extra, for dusting
1 teaspoon xanthan gum
¹/₂ teaspoon salt

1 teaspoon caster sugar
1 teaspoon dried yeast
150 ml (5 fl oz) tepid
  water
1 tablespoon olive oil
polenta (cornmeal), for
  sprinkling

**1** Combine the bread mix, flour, xanthan gum, salt, sugar and yeast in a bowl and make a well in the centre. Pour in the combined water and oil and mix until the dough comes together.

**2** Knead the dough on a surface lightly dusted with brown rice flour for 5 minutes or until smooth. Transfer to a large, lightly oiled bowl and turn to coat in the oil. Cover with plastic wrap and set aside to rise in a warm place for 30 minutes.

**3** Preheat oven to 230°C (450°F/Gas 8). Sprinkle a 23 cm (9 in) pizza tray with polenta.

**4** Punch down the dough in the centre, then roll out on a lightly floured surface to a circle almost large enough to fit the prepared tray. Use your fingers to press the dough out to the edge of the tray. Prick the base with a fork and bake for about 20 minutes.

## indian roti  makes 8

100 g (3¹/₃ oz) amaranth
  flour, plus extra, for
  dusting
100 g (3¹/₃ oz) gluten-
  free cornflour

pinch of salt
150 ml (5 fl oz) water
melted butter, for
  brushing

**1** Put the flours and salt into a bowl and make a well in the centre. Pour in the water and stir until the mixture forms a soft dough.

**2** Gently knead the dough on a surface lightly dusted with amaranth flour for 3 minutes or until smooth. Divide the dough into 8 portions. Roll each portion into a circle.

**3** Put a dough circle in a non-stick fry pan and cook over medium heat until golden, then turn and cook the other side until golden. Use a folded tea towel to press the edge so the roti puffs up. Lightly brush with melted butter and keep warm while you cook the remaining roti.

## savoury shortcrust pastry   makes 1 large pastry case

1/2 cup (60 g/2 oz)
   gluten-free plain flour
   pre-mix
1 1/2 cups (75 g/2 1/2 oz)
   baby rice cereal

125 g (4 oz) cold butter,
   chopped
1 egg white
1–2 tablespoons iced
   water

**1** Put the flour and rice cereal into a bowl. Using your fingertips, rub the butter into the flour mixture until the mixture resembles fine breadcrumbs. Make a well in the centre and stir in the egg white and iced water 1 tablespoon at a time until the pastry comes together. Gather the pastry into a ball and flatten slightly.
**2** Roll out the pastry between 2 sheets of baking paper to line a 20 cm (8 in) ovenproof ceramic or glass pie dish. Trim off any excess pastry. Refrigerate for 20 minutes.
**3** Preheat oven to 200°C (400°F/Gas 6).
**4** Cover the pastry with baking paper and fill with baking beads or uncooked rice. Bake for 15 minutes, then remove the paper and beads or rice and bake for 5 minutes or until golden.

## savoury cheese muffins   makes 12

1 1/2 cups (170 g/5 2/3 oz)
   gluten-free self-raising
   flour
1 cup (150 g/5 oz) fine
   polenta (cornmeal)
1 teaspoon xanthan gum

1/2 cup (60 g/2 oz)
   grated cheddar cheese
1 cup (250 ml/8 fl oz)
   buttermilk
2 eggs, lightly beaten
1/4 cup (60 ml/2 fl oz)
   olive oil

**1** Preheat oven to 200°C (400°F/Gas 6). Line 12 x 1/3 cup (80 ml/2 2/3 fl oz) capacity muffin holes with muffin cases.
**2** Sift the flour and polenta into a bowl and stir in the xanthan gum and cheese. Whisk together the buttermilk, eggs and oil. Pour into the dry ingredients and mix until just combined.
**3** Divide the mixture among the muffin cases and bake for 20 minutes or until risen and golden.

❚ You can also add chopped ham, semi-dried tomatoes, herbs or corn kernels to the mixture.

## savoury biscuits  makes 30

2 cups (240 g/7²/₃ oz)
   gluten-free plain flour
   pre-mix
1 teaspoon gluten-free
   baking powder

¹/₂ teaspoon salt
60 g (2 oz) cold butter,
   chopped
¹/₂ cup (125 ml/4 fl oz)
   iced water

**1**  Preheat oven to 180°C (350°F/Gas 4). Line
2 baking trays with baking paper.
**2**  Sift the flour, baking powder and salt into a bowl.
Using your fingertips, rub the butter into the flour
mixture until the mixture resembles fine breadcrumbs.
**3**  Make a well in the centre and gradually stir in the
water with a flat-bladed knife, using a cutting action,
until the dough comes together. Gather into a ball.
**4**  Roll out half the dough between 2 sheets of
baking paper until 2 mm (¹/₈ in) thick. Using a 6 cm
(2¹/₂ in) cutter, cut out the dough. Place on the
prepared trays and prick all over with a fork. Bake
for 20–25 minutes or until crisp and golden. Transfer
to a wire rack to cool completely. Repeat with the
remaining dough.

▮ You can add 4 tablespoons of sesame seeds,
poppy seeds, grated parmesan cheese or cracked
black pepper to the biscuit mixture.

## crumb coating
makes 1¹/₂ cups

2 cups (60 g/2 oz)
   gluten-free cornflakes
¹/₂ cup (50 g/1²/₃ oz)
   fresh gluten-free
   breadcrumbs

¹/₂ cup (50 g/1²/₃ oz)
   grated parmesan
   cheese
1 tablespoon chopped
   fresh herbs
salt and pepper

**1**  Put the cornflakes into a plastic bag. Using a
rolling pin, lightly crush the cornflakes.
**2**  Transfer the cornflakes to a bowl. Add the
breadcrumbs, parmesan and herbs and season with
salt and pepper. Stir to combine.

▮ The crumb coating must be used immediately or
the cornflakes will soften. Use it to coat chicken,
fish or veal that has been dusted with gluten-free
cornflour and dipped in lightly beaten egg white.
Spray lightly with olive oil spray and bake or grill, or
shallow fry until crisp and golden.

## batter for
## deep frying  makes 1¹/₂ cups

| | |
|---|---|
| 1 cup (120 g/4 oz)<br>  gluten-free plain flour<br>  pre-mix | sea salt and white<br>  pepper<br>1 cup (250 ml/8 fl oz)<br>  soda water |

**1** Sift the flour into a bowl and generously season with sea salt and white pepper.
**2** Add the soda water and whisk until the mixture forms a slightly lumpy batter.

▮ This batter is sufficient to coat 4 pieces of fish. Dip the fish in the batter and deep fry until crisp and golden brown. It also makes a delicious light batter for vegetables or marinated tofu.

## cheese sauce  makes 400 ml

| | |
|---|---|
| 2 tablespoons gluten-<br>  free cornflour<br>400 ml (13 fl oz) milk | ¹/₂ cup (60 g/2 oz)<br>  grated cheddar cheese<br>salt and white pepper |

**1** Blend the cornflour with ¹/₄ cup (60 ml/2 fl oz) of the milk.
**2** Pour the remaining milk into a pan and heat until almost boiling. Remove the pan from the heat and stir in the cornflour mixture. Return to the heat and cook, stirring constantly, over medium heat until the sauce boils and thickens.
**3** Add the cheese and cook, stirring, until the cheese has melted and the sauce has thickened. Season with salt and white pepper.

▮ You can use reduced- or low-fat milk and cheese to lower the fat and calorie content of the sauce. Omit the cheese for a basic white sauce.

## gravy makes 1 cup

1 ½ tablespoons pan
   juices from roast or
   pan fried meat or
   chicken
1 teaspoon gluten-free
   yeast extract spread

2 tablespoons gluten-
   free plain flour pre-mix
1 cup (250 ml/8 fl oz)
   gluten-free chicken
   stock

**1** Remove the meat or chicken from the roasting pan. Add the yeast extract spread and flour and stir to remove any cooked sediment from the base of the roasting pan.
**2** Remove the pan from the heat and gradually add the stock, whisking until smooth.
**3** Return to the heat and cook, stirring constantly, until the gravy boils and thickens.

## stir fry sauce makes ½ cup

2 tablespoons gluten-
   free chicken stock
2 tablespoons gluten-
   free tamari

2 tablespoons gluten-
   free sweet chilli sauce

**1** Whisk together the chicken stock, tamari and sweet chilli sauce.
**2** Pour into a wok and stir over high heat until the sauce boils and thickens.

▮ For a thicker sauce, add 2 teaspoons gluten-free cornflour to the mixture before adding to the wok. The sauce may be added to any meat, vegetable or tofu stir fry.

## biscuit base
makes 1 cheesecake or slice base

200 g (6¹/₂ oz) gluten-
    free cookies, roughly
    crushed
¹/₂ cup (55 g/1²/₃ oz)
    almond meal

60 g (2 oz) butter or
    reduced-fat margarine,
    melted

**1** Put the cookies and almond meal into a food
processor and process until the mixture resembles
fine breadcrumbs. Transfer to a bowl.
**2** Add the melted butter and mix to combine. Press
the mixture over the base of an 18 cm x 28 cm (7 in
x 11 in) cake tin or a 20 cm (8 in) spring form tin.

## sweet shortcrust pastry
makes 8 small or 1 large pastry case

1¹/₂ cups (185 g/6 oz)
    gluten-free cornflour
¹/₄ cup (20 g/³/₄ oz) soy
    flour
¹/₄ cup (35 g/1 oz)
    gluten-free custard
    powder

2 tablespoons caster
    sugar
125 g (4 oz) cold butter,
    chopped
1 egg white
1–2 tablespoons iced
    water

**1** Sift the flours and custard powder into a bowl and
stir in the sugar. Using your fingertips, rub the butter
into the flour mixture until the mixture resembles fine
breadcrumbs. Make a well in the centre and stir in
the egg white and iced water 1 tablespoon at a time
until the pastry comes together. Gather into a ball
and flatten slightly.
**2** Roll out the pastry between 2 sheets of baking
paper to line 8 x 10 cm (4 in) flan tins or a 20 cm
(8 in) ovenproof pie dish. Trim off any excess pastry
with a sharp knife. Refrigerate for 20 minutes.
**3** Preheat oven to 200°C (400°F/Gas 6).
**4** Cover the pastry with baking paper and fill with
baking beads or uncooked rice. Bake for 15 minutes,
then remove the paper and beads or rice and bake
for 5 minutes or until golden.

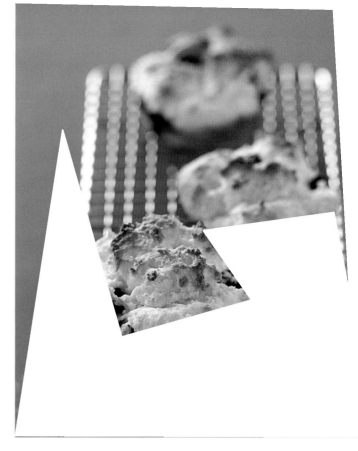

## scones makes 12

2 cups (230 g/7¼ oz)
 gluten-free bread mix
2 cups (320 g/10²/3 oz)
 potato flour, plus
 extra, for dusting
½ cup (70 g/2¼ oz)
 pure icing sugar
1 tablespoon gluten-free
 baking powder
2 teaspoons xanthan gum

1 teaspoon bicarbonate
 of soda (baking soda)
pinch of salt
2 eggs
80 g (2²/3 oz) butter,
 melted
1 cup (250 ml/8 fl oz)
 buttermilk
1 tablespoon buttermilk,
 extra, for brushing

**1** Preheat oven to 220°C (425°F/Gas 7). Line the base of a 20 cm (8 in) square cake tin.
**2** Sift the bread mix, flour, sugar, baking powder, xanthan gum, bicarbonate of soda and salt into a bowl. Whisk together the eggs and butter. Stir into the dry ingredients with a flat-bladed knife, then stir in enough buttermilk to make a soft, sticky dough.
**3** Gently knead the dough on a surface lightly dusted with potato flour; do not overknead. Transfer to the prepared tin and press the dough to fit the tin.
**4** Brush the dough with the extra buttermilk and cut into 12 scones. Bake for 15–18 minutes or until risen and golden. Break into 12 scones and break each in half to serve. The scones can be frozen.

## sweet muffins makes 12

2½ cups (285 g/9 oz)
 gluten-free self-raising
 flour
²/3 cup (170 g/5²/3 oz)
 caster sugar
½ cup (25 g/1 oz) baby
 rice cereal

1 teaspoon xanthan gum
1½ cups (375 ml/
 12 fl oz) buttermilk
2 eggs, lightly beaten
2 tablespoons olive oil

**1** Preheat oven to 200°C (400°F/Gas 6). Grease 12 x ⅓ cup (80 ml/2²/3 fl oz) capacity non-stick muffin holes.
**2** Sift the flour into a bowl and stir in the sugar, rice cereal and xanthan gum. Make a well in the centre. Whisk together the buttermilk, eggs and oil. Pour into the dry ingredients and mix until just combined.
**3** Divide the mixture among the muffin holes and bake for 15–20 minutes or until risen and golden.

▌ To make blueberry muffins, stir 1 cup (160 g/ 5⅓ oz) blueberries into the mixture. For apple and cinnamon muffins, add 100 g (3⅓ oz) apple puree and ½ teaspoon ground cinnamon. For choc chip muffins, stir ½ cup (85 g/2¾ oz) choc chips into the mixture and press ¼ cup (40 g/1⅓ oz) choc chips into the tops of the muffins before baking.

## sponge cake makes 1

3/4 cup (90 g/3 oz)
gluten-free cornflour

2 tablespoons gluten-
free self-raising flour

1 teaspoon cream of
tartar

1/2 teaspoon bicarbonate
of soda (baking soda)

4 eggs, separated

1/2 cup (125 g/4 oz)
caster sugar

2 teaspoons vanilla
essence

**1** Preheat oven to 190°C (375°F/Gas 5). Grease
2 x 22 cm (9 in) deep round cake tins and line with
baking paper.

**2** Sift the flours, cream of tartar and bicarbonate of
soda 3 times.

**3** Whisk the egg whites in a clean, dry bowl until
stiff peaks form. Gradually add the sugar, beating
well after each addition. Add the vanilla and egg
yolks one at a time, beating well after each addition.

**4** Using a metal spoon, gently fold in the sifted dry
ingredients until combined.

**5** Spoon the mixture evenly into the prepared tins
and bake for 18–20 minutes. Set aside for 5 minutes
before turning out on a wire rack to cool. The sponge
cakes can be frozen.

## chocolate cake makes 1

1 1/2 cups (180 g/6 oz)
buckwheat flour

1/2 cup (45 g/1 1/2 oz)
cocoa powder

1 1/2 teaspoons gluten-
free baking powder

1 teaspoon xanthan gum

3/4 cup (185 g/6 oz)
caster sugar

175 g (5 2/3 oz) butter,
melted

1–2 tablespoons milk

3 eggs, lightly beaten

pure icing sugar, for
dusting

**1** Preheat oven to 180°C (350°F/Gas 4). Lightly
grease 2 x 20 cm (8 in) shallow round cake tins.

**2** Sift the flour, cocoa, baking powder and xanthan
gum into a bowl and stir in the caster sugar. Make a
well in the centre.

**3** Whisk together the butter, milk and eggs. Pour
into the well and mix to combine.

**4** Divide the mixture between the prepared tins.
Bake for 20 minutes or until a skewer comes out
clean when inserted into the centre. Set aside for
5 minutes before turning out on a wire rack to cool.
Dust with icing sugar before serving.

▌Try sandwiching the cakes together with chocolate
hazelnut spread, pure fruit spread or cream cheese
sweetened with pure icing sugar.

## pancakes  makes 8

1¹/₂ cups (170 g/5²/₃ oz)
  gluten-free self-raising
  flour
¹/₂ cup (80 g/2²/₃ oz)
  brown rice flour
¹/₃ cup (85 g/2³/₄ oz)
  caster sugar

300 ml (10 fl oz) milk
2 eggs, lightly beaten
60 g (2 oz) butter,
  melted, plus extra,
  for cooking

**1** Sift the flours into a bowl, stir in the sugar and make a well in the centre. Whisk together the milk, eggs and melted butter. Pour into the well and whisk until the batter is smooth.

**2** Lightly grease a non-stick fry pan with a little melted butter. Pour ¹/₄ cup (60 ml/2 fl oz) of the batter into the pan and cook over low-medium heat until bubbles appear on the surface. Turn the pancake over and cook the other side. Keep warm while you cook the remaining batter. Serve the pancakes with pure maple syrup.

## muesli  makes 12 cups

3 cups (90 g/3 oz)
  buckwheat puffs
2 cups (200 g/6¹/₂ oz)
  processed rice bran
2 cups (170 g/5²/₃ oz)
  gluten-free rice flakes
1 cup (120 g/4 oz)
  sultanas

200 g (6¹/₂ oz) dried fruit
  medley
85 g (2³/₄ oz) pepitas
  (pumpkin seeds)
100 g (3¹/₃ oz) puffed
  brown rice

**1** Put all of the ingredients into a large bowl and gently mix to combine.

**2** Transfer the muesli to a large airtight container and seal until ready to use. Store in an airtight container for up to 2 months. Serve with milk and fresh fruit.

# a guide to gluten-free foods

## SAFE FOODS♦

## FOODS TO AVOID♦

Fresh fruit, vegetables, meat, poultry, seafood and eggs are gluten free.

### Flours & grains

Arrowroot ▌ buckwheat ▌ buckwheat flour ▌ chickpea flour (besan) ▌ lentil flour ▌ maize cornflour ▌ pea flour ▌ polenta (cornmeal) ▌ potato flour ▌ quinoa ▌ rice (white and brown) ▌ rice flour ▌ ground rice ▌ rice bran ▌ glutinous rice ▌ sago ▌ tapioca ▌ soy flour ▌ wild rice ▌ gluten-free baking powder

All varieties of wheat including bulgur, couscous, durum, kumat, spelt ▌ wheat starch ▌ wheaten cornflour ▌ wheat flour ▌ multigrain flour ▌ wheatgerm ▌ wheatmeal ▌ wheat bran ▌ semolina ▌ triticale ▌ rye ▌ barley ▌ oats ▌ oatmeal ▌ oat bran ▌ malt ▌ baking powder

### Cereals

Non-malted rice or corn breakfast cereals ▌ baby rice cereal ▌ gluten-free pasta ▌ rice noodles ▌ rice vermicelli

Wheat-based and mixed-grain breakfast cereals ▌ muesli ▌ rolled oats ▌ baby cereals (except rice) ▌ pasta ▌ noodles ▌ vermicelli

### Breads, biscuits, cakes & pastries

Gluten-free breads ▌ taco shells ▌ white corn tortillas ▌ rice cakes and crackers (plain) ▌ gluten-free biscuits, cakes and pastries

All breads, biscuits, cakes and pastries containing wheat, rye, barley or oats ▌ sourdough commercial breads

### Dairy & soy products

Milk ▌ calcium-fortified soy milk ▌ baby formula ▌ most yoghurts ▌ cheese ▌ plain ice cream ▌ tofu

Malted milk ▌ flavoured milk ▌ custard powder ▌ soy milk with malt/maltodextrin

### Jams, spreads & condiments

Jam ▌ marmalade ▌ honey ▌ golden syrup ▌ maple syrup ▌ peanut butter ▌ herbs ▌ spices ▌ curry powder ▌ gluten-free tamari

Vegemite ▌ Marmite ▌ Promite ▌ commercial relishes, chutneys and mustards ▌ soy sauce

### Beverages

Water ▌ rice milk ▌ mineral water ▌ soda water ▌ tonic water ▌ fruit juice ▌ soft drinks ▌ tea ▌ coffee ▌ wine ▌ liqueurs ▌ spirits

Coffee substitutes ▌ drinking chocolate ▌ malted drinks ▌ oat milk ▌ lemon barley ▌ beers and ales

♦ Always check the ingredients of packaged and processed foods as ingredients may vary between manufacturers. Contact the Coeliac Society of Australia (see page 128) if you are unsure of any ingredient.

# gluten-free glossary

## almond meal

Also known as ground almonds, almond meal is made from blanched almonds that have been ground into a fine powder or meal. It makes a great low-GI substitute for flour in baking recipes, producing a slightly denser finished product. Almond or hazelnut meal is the main ingredient in flourless chocolate cakes. Store it in the refrigerator or freezer to prevent it from turning rancid.

## amaranth flour

A strongly flavoured, brownish-coloured flour, amaranth is best used in combination with other flours. It has a high nutrient value and should be stored in an airtight container in the refrigerator. Because of its strong flavour, it is best used in baked chocolate or spiced recipes. Available in health-food shops.

## arrowroot

Produced from the root of a starchy tuber, arrowroot can be used to thicken sauces and gravies, making it a good, tasteless substitute for gluten-free cornflour. Blend it with a little water before adding it to sauces. It can also be used in baking and works to lighten the finished product.

## baby rice cereal

Baby rice cereal is a versatile ingredient used widely in gluten-free cooking to help lighten breads and add crispness to cookies and pastries. For those watching their weight, it can be used to replace almond meal or coconut in recipes. However, baby rice cereal is a high-GI food.

## brown rice flour

A soft, versatile flour, brown rice flour is suitable for all types of gluten-free baking. It has more fibre than white rice flour and is great to use in pancakes, biscuits and cakes.

## buckwheat flour

Buckwheat flour is a nutty-flavoured, highly nutritious flour that can be used to enrich most baked products. It is best used in combination with other flours.

## chickpea flour (besan)

This golden-coloured flour is used widely in Indian cooking to make batters. It is best used in baking in combination with other flours, and is especially good to use when making muffins and cakes. It contains more protein, fibre and folate than wheat flour.

## gluten-free baking powder

Gluten-free baking powder is clearly marked and available in supermarkets. However, do not assume all baking powder is gluten free. To add rise to 1 cup of homemade gluten-free flour mix, add 1 teaspoon cream of tartar and 1/2 teaspoon bicarbonate of soda (baking soda).

## gluten-free bread mix

This pre-mix is made up of gluten-free cornflour, rice flour, bicarbonate of soda (baking soda) and guar gum. It is suitable for use in bread makers and is available in supermarkets and health-food shops.

## gluten-free cornflour

Also known as cornstarch, maize flour or maize starch, cornflour is a soft, silky flour used widely in gluten-free cooking. It can be blended with water and used to thicken sauces and gravies, and used in batters and coatings for fried foods. It is the main ingredient in gluten-free flour pre-mixes. Check the ingredients carefully, as some packaged cornflour is made from wheat and contains gluten.

## gluten-free custard powder

Custard powder adds sweetness and colour to baked goods. Check the ingredients carefully, as some brands are based on wheat flour and are not gluten free.

## gluten-free flour mixes

Widely available in supermarkets and health-food shops, these ready-combined gluten-free flour mixes make an excellent substitute for flour. Most commercial mixes consist of a combination of gluten-free cornflour, tapioca flour and rice flour. Gluten-free self-raising flour has had a raising agent added to the mix.

## gluten-free rice flakes

These rolled flakes of rice make a perfect substitute for rolled oats in porridge. They are firmer than traditional rolled oats and can be soaked in water or milk before use to soften them. The flakes can also be used in muesli, anzac biscuits or in coatings for chicken and fish.

## gluten-free tamari

Tamari is a gluten-free soy sauce made without using wheat in the fermentation process. Check the ingredients carefully as some manufacturers include wheat in tamari. Available in health-food shops.

## hazelnut meal

Ground hazelnuts can be used as you would use almond meal as a replacement for flour in baked cakes. They are especially good with chocolate. Store ground nut meals in an airtight container in the freezer to prevent them from turning rancid. Replacing nut meals for flour will significantly increase the kilojoule content of a recipe. However, it may also lower the GI level and add fibre.

## polenta (cornmeal)

Made of ground corn, polenta is available as coarse or fine, the latter being more suitable for baking. Polenta is perfect in muffins, scones, breads, pancakes and pizza bases. It can also be used to bind mixtures.

## potato flour

Potato flour is a good, all-round, soft flour that is suitable for both baking and thickening. It is best used in combination with other higher fibre flours.

## pure icing sugar

Unlike icing sugar mixture, which often contains wheaten cornflour, pure icing sugar is gluten free. Store it in an airtight container, as it will harden if it comes into contact with any moisture.

## soy flour

Soy flour is a golden-coloured, high-fibre flour with a strong, distinctive taste. It is best used in combination with other flours, particularly brown rice flour, and has a higher fat content than other flours. It should be stored in an airtight container in the refrigerator.

## tapioca flour

A silky, white flour that can be used as a substitute for arrowroot, tapioca flour provides lightness to the finished product and is perfect for batters or coatings. It is slightly rubbery in texture, and may also be used to thicken sauces and gravies.

## white rice flour

This heavy flour is less nutritious than brown rice flour. It is best known for its use in Asian cooking, where it is used to make rice noodles. Often used to make shortbread and biscuits, it is best used in combination with other flours. Rice flour is a major ingredient in commercial gluten-free breads.

## xanthan gum food additive (415)

The wonder ingredient when it comes to gluten-free baking, xanthan gum is used to replace the structural function of gluten and helps prevent gluten-free baked goods from crumbling and falling apart. Use 1/2 teaspoon xanthan gum in a cake mixture, 1 teaspoon for pastry and 1 tablespoon for a loaf of bread. Be sure to add it to the dry ingredients before adding the liquid. Available in the health-food section of major supermarkets or in health-food shops.

## yeast

Check the ingredients carefully — most yeasts are gluten free but there are a few that are made using wheat flour. Instant dried yeast is the best kind to use in gluten-free baking.

# index

recipes & styling **Jody Vassallo**

baking recipes **Dianne Boyle**

photographer **Sue Ferris**

food for photography **Abi Ulgiati,**

    **Wendy Quisumbing**

recipe testing **Danieka Cottrell**

props stylist **Carlu Seaver**

details styling **Abi Ulgiati**

designer **Annette Fitzgerald**

introduction **Dr Kim Faulkner-Hogg**

editor **Justine Harding**

consultant dietitian **Dr Susanna Holt**

Special thanks to Judy Clarke for the great carrot and walnut muffins, brandy walnut cake and all the other yummy recipes she contributed. Also thanks to Sabrina for her amazing Brazilian cheese balls, and Di Boyle for the great bread and baking recipes. A super huge thank you to my partners Claire, Helen and Peter for trusting me on this one. Thanks to Annette for her wonderful design and input. Thanks to my photographic team for making every day at work a living, laughing joy. And finally thanks to Justine, my incredible pregnant editor, who took us to the finish line on this one – we couldn't have done it without you.

## Styling Credits

Accoutrement (02) 9969 1031 ▮ Alfresco Emporium (02) 9999 4299 ▮ Antique General Store (02) 9913 7636 ▮ Beclau (02) 9698 6422 www.beclau.com ▮ Bison (02) 6257 7255 www.bisonhome.com ▮ Country Road Home 1800 801 911 www.countryroad.com.au ▮ Design Mode International (02) 9998 8200 ▮ Dinosaur Designs (02) 9698 3500 www.dinosaurdesigns.com.au ▮ Ginger Flower (02) 8920 3199 ▮ Grok (02) 9908 5411 www.grok.com.au ▮ Mud Australia (02) 9699 7600 www.mudaustralia.com ▮ Papaya (02) 9386 9980 www.papaya.com.au ▮ Pulp Creative Paper (02) 9976 6688 ▮ Rapee (02) 9496 4511 www.rapee.com.au ▮ Rhubarb (03) 9681 9922 www.rhubarb.net.au ▮ Riedel Glassware 1300 780 124 info@ambient.com.au ▮ Riess Enamelware www.goldfishent.com ▮ The Essential Ingredient (02) 9550 5477 ▮ Villa Homewares 1800 443 366 www.gcmpoliving.com.au ▮ Wheel & Barrow (02) 9938 4555 www.wheelandbarrow.com.au ▮ Your Display Gallery (02) 9906 7556 ▮ Appliances used in this book provided by Sunbeam Corporation Limited.

This edition published in 2008 by **GRUB STREET** 4 Rainham Close, London SW11 6SS

email: food@grubstreet.co.uk   www.grubstreet.co.uk

ISBN 978-1-904943-67-9

Printed in India.

DISCLAIMER: The nutritional information listed under each recipe does not include the nutrient content of garnishes or any accompaniments or ingredients not listed in specific quantities in the ingredient list. The nutritional information for each recipe is an estimate only, and may vary depending on the brand of ingredients used, and due to natural biological variations in the composition of natural foods such as meat, fish, fruit and vegetables. The nutritional information was calculated by a qualified dietitian using FoodWorks dietary analysis software (Professional Version 3.10, Xyris Software Pty Ltd, Highgate Hill, Queensland, Australia) based on the Australian food composition tables and food manufacturers' data. Where not specified, ingredients are analysed as average or medium. If more than one option is given for an ingredient, the analysis is based on an average of the ingredients. All recipes were analysed using 59 g eggs.

An approximate glycemic index (GI) rating is also listed under the nutrient information for each recipe to indicate whether the dish produces a low, medium or high blood glucose response. The GI categories (low, medium or high) listed for each recipe are estimates only and were calculated by an experienced dietitian using published GI values for each of the carbohydrate-containing ingredients in the recipe. If an ingredient didn't have a published GI value, the GI value of the most similar foodstuff was used as a substitute. For this reason, and the fact that food preparation and cooking methods can affect a food's GI value, it is not possible to estimate the GI value of a recipe exactly.

This book is intended to provide general information only regarding wheat- and gluten-free diets and is not intended to replace any medical advice given to you by a qualified health professional. The authors and publisher cannot be held responsible for any adverse effects resulting from the use or misuse of the recommendations in this book or the failure to obtain or take appropriate medical advice.

IMPORTANT: Those who might suffer particularly adverse effects from salmonella food poisoning (the elderly, pregnant women, young children and those with immune system problems) should consult their general practitioner about consuming raw or undercooked eggs.